Wakeboarding
...On the Edge

By
Jason Weber

Sports ...on the Edge
P.O. Box 931
Mays Landing NJ 08330

International Standard Book Number: 0-9676408-0-6

Printed and bound in the United States of America.

Note: This publication contains the opinions and ideas of its author. It is intended to provide helpful and informative material on the subject matter covered. It is sold with the understanding that the author and publisher are not responsible for any individual's actions taken as a result of material covered. The author and publisher specifically disclaim any responsibility for any liability, loss or risk, personal or otherwise, which is incurred as a consequence, directly or indirectly, of the use and application of any of the contents of this book.

Production Team:
Jason Weber - *Project leader; Author*
Chris Polk - *Lead photographer*
Brandy Cross - *Photographer*
Jamie Haughee - *Page layout, graphics and cover design*
Leah M. Pennington - *Copy editor; consultant*

Participating Athletes:
Maeghan Major, Dana Preble, Gerry Nunn, Stevie Williams (cover), Jennifer Hathaway, Jenn Elbon, Kimi Tran, Todd Testa, Judy Testa, Mark Cohen, Jim Rodeo, Jason Weber, Bart Copeland, Drew Dill, Mike McLin, Jeff Taylor, Alan Booth, Mike Leiffers, Henrich Rian, Eric Shamas.

P.O. Box 491
Longport, NJ 08403

P.O. Box 931
Mays Landing, NJ 08330

4615 Milford Ct.
Fort Wayne, IN 46816

ACKNOWLEDGEMENTS

First off, I need to thank my family, who have often wondered if I was still a member during this project, but supported me nonetheless; My "partners" in the project - Arnaud Voermans, who understood what I wanted to accomplish with the CDROM and delivered it exactly how I had seen it in my mind's eye - Chris Polk, who's mastery of photography and unique personality make photo shoots much more productive and entertaining; My advisors and close friends: Mark Cohen, for helping out with just about everything, including my sanity; Eric Meyer, for steering me in the right direction with the print product; Much thanks goes out to the people who have helped me throughout the years, specifically: Kelley Woolsey & Jennifer Leachman, Scott Callahan, and especially Patricia Luderitz (Grandmom), also Kyle Cinami at Neptune, who has always lent a helping hand, and provided me with access to some of the best athletes in the world for this project, Paul O'Brien and the entire crew at Hyperlite for their longstanding and continued support; John "JT" Thomas for his technical expertise and resourcefulness in producing this product; All of the athletes who participated in this project who are named in the previous page for all the early photo shoots and who graciously fulfilled my demands. I also need to thank all of the athletes who have taught me what I have learned over the past ten years as well as the students who have served as inspiration for writing this title.

Getting Started

Safety

One thing that cannot be overstressed in this sport is the importance of safety. Boats, boards, ropes, propellers, fins and "big air" can all cause serious injuries and even death if you don't use common sense. Although we will be discussing some particular techniques to avoid injuries while riding, it is your responsibility to know the rules of the water and abide by them. Do not use this book as your sole source of safety information. You will also want check with your local authorities for specific information regarding boating laws in your state or region.

Equipment Safety

The use of a United States Coast Guard (USCG) approved lifejacket is highly recommended for several reasons. First and most importantly, you could find that a lifejacket will actually save your life. So, it is important that your vest fits properly or it won't serve its purpose. Second, they're required by law in many states. Complying with this law will save you the hassle of dealing with "the man" and cost of hefty fines. Third, lifejackets can buffer the immense pain you will inevitably feel when taking a bad fall. And finally, you will get less tired, ride longer and practice more since you won't have to waste time and energy swimming after each fall. If you think that the pros don't wear lifejackets during practice and decide they're not for you either, think again. Check with any of the big name wakeboarders like Dean Lavelle or Shaun Murray on how they outfit themselves when training. They have been known to wear several wetsuits along with bulky lifejackets at the same time for protection when learning new moves.

Although it's recommended that you always wear a USCG-approved lifejacket, some riders opt for the slimmer and more comfortable versions of the neoprene flotation vests. While these vests will keep you from tiring as easily, you may risk the possibility of drowning if knocked unconscious. Some of the new non-approved flotation vests and wetsuits are shaped and padded to soften the blow of harder falls.

Always make sure that you check all of your equipment thoroughly, including tightening all binding and fin bolts. Remember, a quick check of the thumbscrews on your bindings could save you a broken leg.

Driving Safety

As stated earlier, it is best to refer to your local authorities for unique boating laws regarding towables behind boats. Another good source of information and general rules of the waterways is the well-known *Chapman's Piloting*. It's information is indispensable, and is a great reference for those times when you may wonder about specific boating guidelines.

Terminology & Wake Speak

Many riders, especially those new to the sport, often find it difficult to understand the lingo involved with wakeboarding. This can make it hard to learn new moves that an instructor or video describes. Often beginners find it a little embarrassing to ask what a word or term means. So, to get you started, the following list includes some of the most commonly used terms and their meanings.

Edge This term has a couple of meanings. As a noun, it is most commonly used to describe the lengthwise profile of the board, and is sometimes referred to as the "rail".

Mark edges toward the wake

There are technical differences between these two terms, however they are beyond the scope of this book.

As a verb, it describes the action of having less of the surface of the board on the water by setting the board on its edge as described above.

Leading & Trailing Edge The leading edge of the board is the one that is closest to the boat. The trailing edge is the one furthest from the boat.

Heelside or Backside Determined by your back or heels facing the wake while riding in a straight line outside the wake. (Fig.1) Used to describe a rider's approach style to the wake, i.e. "He did an awesome backside roll!"

Toeside or Frontside Determined by your chest or toes facing the wake while riding in a straight line outside the wake. (Fig. 2) i.e. "Did you see that huge frontside front flip?"

Left Foot Forward & Right Foot Forward
This describes the foot closest to the tow boat. It can be determined by observing which foot you put into your pants first. This is usually the easiest way to determine your natural foot forward.

Regular Foot Describes a rider whose natural stance is to ride with the left foot forward.

Goofy Foot Describes a rider whose natural stance is to ride with the right foot forward.

Revert, Switchstance, Fakie These terms mean the same thing and describe riding in the position that is opposite your natural stance. For instance, "revert" for a left foot forward rider, would be right foot forward and vise versa.

Half - Cab Describes initiating a trick from the "fakie" or "revert" position and landing in the normal or natural foot forward position.

Boat Wake The following is a diagram of the different sections of a wake

Equipment & Setup

The beginner will need to thoroughly cover all of the equipment involved before the first ride. This section will be split into two parts, one covering the materials you will be directly connected to while riding, including boards, bindings, rope, accessories, and how to configure them properly. The second section will discuss the other equipment and setup involved with riding, including tow vehicles, extended pylons and how to increase the size of the wake for big air.

Choosing A Board

Today there is a myriad of wakeboards to choose from. There are boards for each different rider's size, riding style and ability. The details of all the different board shapes and characteristics are entirely too much to surmise in only a few pages, so it's a good idea to consult your favorite wakeboard retailer to determine which board will suit you best. Here are a few general rules of thumb when choosing:

Board size is mostly based on the rider's weight. The heavier the rider, the bigger the board needs to be.

If you are sharing the board with others, buy the board that fits the heaviest rider or the rider who will be using it most often.

Determining Left Foot Forward (LFF) vs. Right Foot Forward (RFF) Many wakeboarders have had experience in other sports such as skateboarding, surfing, and snowboarding and will already know which foot they prefer to have forward. If you are a beginner with no board-sport experience, you will first need to determine whether you are a "Regular Foot" or a "Goofy Foot" rider. If you have ever ridden a skateboard, you can determine this by knowing that you push with your rear foot while the front foot stays on the board for balance. Another way to tell which foot forward a person should ride is to have them stand in front of you without telling them what you're doing. Have the new rider stand facing away from you on flat, level ground with nothing in front of him. Now, while paying close attention to his feet, give him a firm push at the top of the back as if you are trying to make him fall. In most cases the new rider will catch himself with the foot he will use as the back foot. The foot that stayed in place will be the front foot. For example if you are a left foot forward or "Regular Foot" rider, you will catch your fall with the right foot.

If these techniques don't work and all else fails, simply try each stance and stick with the one that works best and is most comfortable.

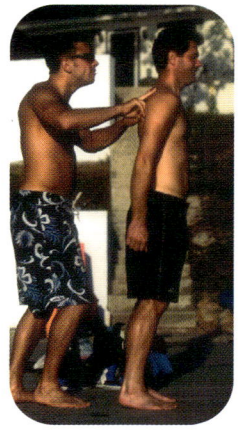
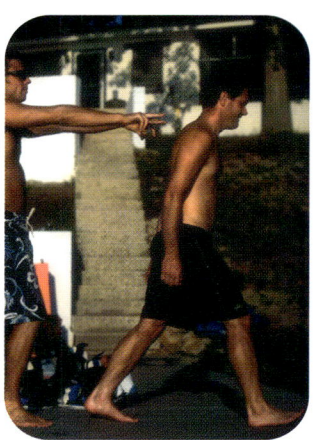

Stance Width & Angle Demystified

Stance width is one of the most common questions asked, and at the same time it is one of the most ignored subjects of riders of all abilities. Here is how stance width works, the closer your feet are together, the less stable you will be during landings, while the wider the stance, the more stable your landings will be. You can test this theory by having a friend push you from the side with your feet together and then with your feet spread far apart.

(Make sure that it is a friend who is pushing you, and not the guy you jumped over at the lake last weekend, or he might not be very gentle in this experiment.)

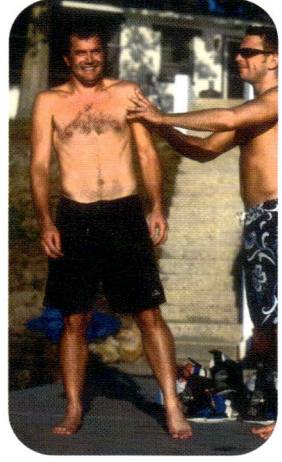

Obviously you want to be as stable as possible, so one would assume that you should make your stance as wide as you can stretch your legs, right? Wrong. The reason you shouldn't use an incredibly wide stance is because you will be sacrificing the amount of spring or "pop" off of the wake as you go for air. And it can be uncomfortable. Compare jumping off the top of a wake to any other kind of jumping. If you were to try to jump up and touch a basketball rim, how would you do

it? Would your feet be spread out extra wide? Would your feet and knees be touching together? No. Think about why. If you have your feet spread out super wide, you would lose that critical bit of springiness to get the height you need. If your feet were touching together, you might topple over a bit and lose your balance as you land. Therefore the best recommendation is to keep your feet just slightly wider than shoulder width apart. This will give you enough width to keep you stable when you land, while retaining the ability to get a good "pop" off of the wake.

This method works for most people. However, you will want to determine and then use your own personal preference. A good test to find the most comfortable stance width for you is to jump off of a low platform (3 steps high or so), when

you land, take note of how wide your stance width is, this is most likely your natural width. You will also want to take note of how your feet are angled.

The angle that your feet (bindings) are placed also tends to be misunderstood quite a bit. Many people think that riding with a "duck" stance will enable them to ride switchstance better. This is not necessarily the case. The purpose of an angle on the stance is to help the body and shoulders open up to the boat so that they don't have to twist as much. The rule here again is comfort and personal preference based on some simple guidelines. When your feet are at a zero degree angle or "squared up", you will be able to get the most out of your edge to the wake. Your toes will actually "dig" into the water deeper when on your toeside edge. You may find that you are more stable riding switchstance or "switch" with a zero rear foot angle, because your rear foot has more of the board's width under control.

A good starting point for stance angles would be to set your natural front foot at either nine or eighteen degrees forward, and your rear foot at zero degrees. (Fig. 1) As you get comfortable with riding, refer to how your feet were angled during the jumping experiment and change the stance to suit you. Riders are rarely set up with anything more than 18 (front)/-18 (rear) degrees on either foot. (Fig. 2) Another reason to avoid the 45/-45 stance angle types is injury to your knees. When you place your

feet at these angles it's difficult to bend your knees. Many snowboarders have learned this lesson the hard way by blowing-out their knees on harsh landings using this stance. Try doing the basketball rim experiment with these angles along with the different stance widths as well. You will find that you cannot jump as high with the extreme stance angles. And with an extremely wide stance, you will be lucky to jump at all. The step-jumping test is probably the best to determine both your stance width and angle. If you find that you land from the jump test or walk with a bit of a "duck" foot or stance, go for it on the wakeboard as well. Just remember to use some common sense and think logically about any trends you might have heard of. Just because they look cool or unique, does not always mean they actually work.

Binding Fit & Function

BINDING MODELS AND STYLES VARY FROM MANUFACTURERS, THEREFORE IT IS EXTREMELY IMPORTANT THAT YOU CONSULT AND ADHERE TO THE RECOMMENDATIONS PROVIDED BY THE DOCUMENTATION ENCLOSED WITH YOUR PARTICULAR PRODUCT. THE FOLLOWING INFORMATION IS MERELY A GUIDELINE, AND NOT GOSPEL.

For the most part, the old style bungee binding is rarely used today. Many price point wakeboards come standard with bungee bindings due to the advantage of the adjustability of fitting the binding to the rider. This is ideal for a family or group of riders new to the sport who plan to share the same board. The proper way to fit the bungee binding is to start by adjusting the top footstrap so that it is snug over the front of the

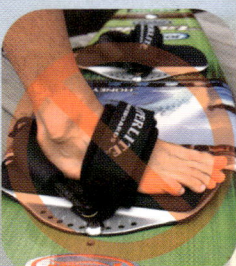

foot, almost covering your toes. Also, make sure that it won't let your foot slide forward allowing the strap to get closer to the bottom of your shin.

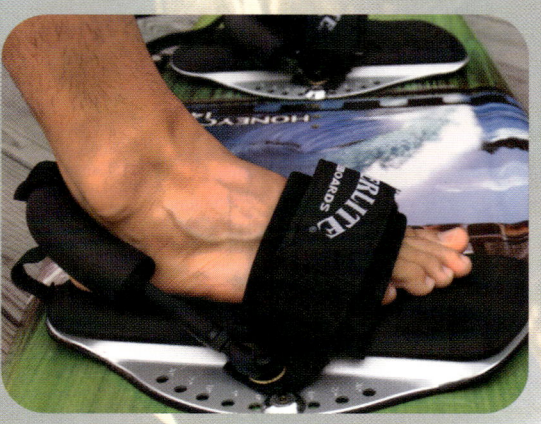

Boot style bindings have become much more popular due to their increased performance characteristics. The fit of the boot should be snug, but not overly tight. Some riders prefer them tighter than others, and many boots have certain areas to adjust for a more custom fit. The thing to keep in mind when fitting and adjusting your bindings is the actual function. They are designed to release your foot from the boot after a fall. Make sure the two boots are fitted to the same tightness. When you fall you either want both feet in the boots, or both feet out. If one foot is in the boot and the other is out, the board can twist in any direction and has enough leverage to tweak your foot in many painful and dangerous ways, potentially leaving you injured.

Getting Into & Out of Your Boots

While most boot manufacturers discourage the use of them for legal reasons, many people prefer to use some type of lubricant to help them get their foot into the boot more easily. Liquid dish soap tends to be the most popular lube to use. Unfortunately dish soap destroys the rubber materials over a period of time. Commercial brands of binding lube are available that won't damage your equipment, and tend to rinse out more quickly. However they can be more expensive.

Judy holds Duck Butter, her choice for binding lube.

Shaving cream has become the lube choice for many riders because it rinses out quicker than soap, is cheaper, more readily available than commercially branded binding lubes and feels good getting into - plus it makes your feet smell good! But, it too has the drawback of slowly eating away at your boots.

Removing boots at the end of a ride can be a tricky task for anyone. So the best way for you, the new rider to remove boots, is to simultaneously grab the edge of the board at your toes with both hands. From this position pull the board's edge toward you.

As you gain more experience using your boots you will find that there are other practical ways to remove them including:

🔶 Sink the board underneath you so that you are directly over top of it. Push down with one foot while lifting the heel and yanking up with the other. Once one foot is free, place it between the boots then push with the free foot and pull with the other.

🔶 In shallow water, stand on top of the board until it gets stuck to the bottom and literally jump out of the boots.

Ropes & Handles

The use of a "non-stretch" rope is imperative to this sport. It will not only reduce the chances of the handle recoiling back into the boat, potentially hitting people or breaking windshields, but it will actually help you get more "load" on the line (explained later) and consequently bigger air.

When it comes to handles, the wider the better. Wider handles will enable a rider to be more stable and the extra space to grab makes learning handle pass tricks much easier.

This board uses a two-inch cleaver fin.

Fin Setup

Fin setup can be a confusing ordeal at times, especially for riders new to the sport. You should experiment with different sizes and shapes of fins to improve your performance and change the riding characteristics of the board. However, keep it simple and follow what works. For ideas, research what the pros are riding on. You will find that most are riding with a single two inch "ramp" style fin on each end of the board. Some of the hottest new boards available use two smaller fins on each end. This setup tends to be the choice of those who ride more wake to wake, versus taking long cuts and landing in the flats.

Mike grabs Indy on his four fin board.

Fly Advice

🔶 Use a smaller fin (1.5") for lighter riders and those who are less aggressive.

🔶 Use a larger fin (2.5") for riders over 200 pounds or extremely rough water conditions.

🔶 Use a smaller fin when you have trouble with surface maneuvers. They make it easier for the fin to release from it's track.

Boats & "Riding Enhancement" Accessories

One of the main reasons wakeboarding is becoming extremely popular is its accessibility to a variety of different groups of people. Because of a board's width, it requires less energy to get up and riding for both the rider and the boat pulling him. Just about any water vehicle with more than ten horsepower can pull an average sized rider. Although this horsepower level may be less than ideal, it is possible. This versatility has brought new riders into the sport who, as they get more involved, grow into more powerful and higher quality tow vehicles. The advent of the three-person personal watercraft has also helped the sport attract a variety of riders as well. Teens through mid twenty year olds who can't afford a $30,000 boat are using this option. You can spend $6,000 on a brand new personal watercraft and have an excellent tow vehicle with little maintenance costs. Of course the ideal tow vehicle is the tournament quality inboards that you see at the X-games and at the pro tour stops. These boats are weighted down to create larger wakes, have the "tuna towers" to tie their rope to and 300 plus horsepower engines that can move it all. The following information discusses how all of those things can help you have fun and get bigger air.

Tournament Inboards

Obviously the most sought after tow vehicles for wakeboarding are ones designed specifically for the sport. Tournament quality inboards are known for their unique handling characteristics, easy maintenance procedures, and famously consistent wakes. Inboards also tend to do a significantly better job at holding steady speeds, especially those speeds used for wakeboarding. Since there are few adjustments that can be made with inboards, driving and weight distribution are relatively uncomplicated.

Tournament Inboard with a "Tuna Tower"

Outboards & Stern Drives (I/Os)

While outboards and stern drives are not as easy to perfect at first, with a little experimentation and careful note taking you can figure out how to dial in wakes exactly to your specs every time. Stern drives and outboards with power trim give the driver a multitude of options when it comes to forming the wake. Often there are several variables to remember, so keeping a record for each different variable that you try is a must.

Whether you have an outboard with weight in the back or it's relatively empty, try trimming down to get the nose down and the boat to plane. Doing this will help the driver keep a more consistent speed as well. Of course you will be sacrificing wake size for the boat's performance characteristics. When the boat is trimmed down, the boat is essentially pushing less water and creating less of a wake, while the opposite applies with a higher trim.

Motor trim up

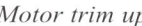
Motor trim down

Ideally you would want to have enough weight placed towards the front of the boat to keep the nose down, while keeping the trim up slightly to push some water and create a decent wake.

Since stern drives have a heavier inboard style engine in the back, you will probably find it necessary to knock the trim down more than you typically would for an outboard. These I/Os also tend to have wakes that spread further apart at a shorter distance from the boat, so you will want to keep a log of what rope length works best for each trim position.

Personal Water Craft (PWC)

A PWC won't provide the huge wakes that advanced riders desire, but the larger new three person designs have enough power to get you around the lake. Surprisingly enough PWCs can get you in the air with their wakes, although they will be smaller than wakes from a full size boat.

Weighting the Boat Down

Some riders put lead weights in their boat, fill waterbed bladders or recruit ten times the maximum legal limit of passengers in their boat just to add more weight. The reason? The more weight you have in the boat, the more water it will displace creating larger wakes and bigger air. You may be wondering what method works the best to weigh down your boat, however, recommending one over another is simply a matter of utility. On the one hand lead bars work really well. They are small and can be tucked away on the sides of the gunnels or in the bow and allow for more room to move in the boat. Solid weights like lead bars make adjusting the wakes a little easier as well. Water bags are also a good option especially if you trailer your boat on a regular basis. Pumping the water in and out can save wear and tear on both your trailer and towing vehicle and it's essentially hassle-free. Another good idea is to go to your local hardware store and purchase five-inch PVC pipes. Begin by cutting them down to a manageable size, fill the pipes with wet sand and complete by capping off the ends. Then place the tubes where necessary in the boat. No matter what type of weight you use, be sure to stay within the boat's maximum recommended and legal weight capacity.

Always use weights properly. Using weights with a beginner or timid rider behind the boat is not suggested because it will make things more difficult for the new rider.

White wash can make it difficult for novices to cross wakes.

Often times a beginner will ride at a slower speed. This combined with extra weight will cause a sloppy wake that will eventually swamp the rider. For more experienced riders, you will probably want to put as much weight as possible in the boat to increase the wake size. Keep in mind that you can add too much weight and it is possible to make the wake larger than what even an experienced rider can handle. As a rider, if you have an incredibly huge wake and run the same short line that you have been using with the smaller wake you will be in for a big surprise. You may quickly find that you lose your speed as you travel up the wake and won't land out as far into the flats. The solution for this is to make the line longer. This will give you more time to set up for your move and adequate distance from the wake to generate speed. You will also need to increase the boat speed with a longer line because you will find that the wakes are mushy when you are back this far. Increasing the boat speed will make the wakes firmer and give you something a little more solid to spring off of. Ever jump on a bed as a kid? Fun right? Now imagine trying to jump on a waterbed. It's not possible because there is nothing firm to push from. Those examples all share the same theory.

Make sure the boat is evenly weighted on each side. If the boat is not balanced correctly, the wakes will become uneven. Few things are as annoying as a disproportionate wake for the rider. To balance the wakes, have the rider move to the center of the wake while driving at normal riding speed. If one of the wakes does not have a smooth edge and the other does you will need to balance the boat. To properly balance the boat move the weight to the side that has the wash rolling down it.

Continue to move the weights until both sides maintain a similar smooth face.

Uneven wakes; shift weight to left side.

Smooth, even wakes.

Keep in mind that the more weight you have towards the back of the boat, the bigger and steeper the wakes will become. However, large wakes are a trade-off with boat handling. When the majority of the weight is placed in the rear of the boat, the nose will rise high during initial acceleration, you may have difficulty getting planed off, and it can be very difficult to steer. When you distribute the weight evenly from front to back you should have a reasonable trade-off between wake size and boat handling.

Pylons, Extended Pylons, Tuna Towers, Etc…

So you may be wondering why towboats have tall poles or pylons in them. The function of these pylons is to give riders the ability to tie-off higher up, giving them a number of advantages. The main advantage is the upward pull. Instead of being pulled *across* the water, the extra height gives the rider more of an upward pull. This upward tug can help you survive sketchy landings or serve as a handicap for you when learning new moves. The shorter the rope is the more of a direct upward pull or angle you will receive. In the following chapters you will learn how to use this upward pull to your advantage when practicing new moves or teaching beginners how to get up. The extra height does not necessarily make you jump higher, but it does not pull you back down like those ropes tied off low. In fact, you actually get a little more "hang time" when in the air without being hindered from going higher.

How is the extended pylon different from the "tuna towers"? The extended pylon was the first generation of high tie-offs and is the most cost-effective way to do so. These pylons cost approximately $300 to $350 depending on they style and quality. Although the extended pylons work very well for their price, more advanced riders and experienced drivers will tell you that there are some drawbacks. One such drawback is that when a rider is pulling hard out to one side, the extra leverage that the high pole creates on the boat causes the boat to tilt unnaturally (also called "listing"). This makes it difficult to steer, hold a steady speed and may significantly affect the wake by flattening it out on the side that the rider will be approaching. Some riders also feel that the extended poles feel a bit "spongy" as they are edging toward the wake. This is most likely due to a front anchor strap not being tight enough, but can also be caused by the excess leverage the pole puts on the boat.

"Tuna Towers" are becoming increasing popular and aren't often considered a novelty item any longer by experienced drivers or riders. The towers effectively eliminate all of the drawbacks associated with extended pylons. Due to the four anchor points on the tower there is no flex from a single pole, no straps to tighten and less "listing". These towers are of course more costly with a price tag of about $1,200. However, these towers are the ultimate space saving accessory. Not only do they let you tie-off high, but they allow the use of the rear seats in the boat. And there are plenty of aftermarket pieces you can purchase to store your boards or mount high-powered lights and boombastic speaker systems. The best part is that you can attach or mount each accessory on the tower and out of the way.

First Time Techniques
and Fundamentals

Getting up the first time

Dry Land Training

You will want to start with some practice on the land before you actually get in the water. Start by grabbing a partner and a tow handle. Have your partner hold the handle by the "V" while you hang on to the bar itself. Sit on the ground with your knees bent halfway up to your chest. Now grab the handle with a "palms down" grip as wide as the handle will allow. (Fig. 1) The wider the grip, the more stable you will be when riding. This also makes it easier and more comfortable to hang on to while riding with the opposite foot forward. This type of grip will keep your body balanced, whereas a baseball grip actually gives you a favored or stronger pull on one side. Keep your arms straight with your elbows just hugging around the top of your knees.

Now have your partner pull you up. Let him do all of the work. (Fig. 2) Make sure that you keep your arms straight and do not pull yourself up. (Fig. 3) As your partner pulls, you should slide your butt toward your heels before actually rising off the floor. When you rise you will want to end up standing with your knees slightly bent and your arms straight. Focus on being pulled up by your hips, not your shoulders. Practice this technique a few times until you get it perfect and it becomes natural to you.

In the Water

Getting up on a wakeboard is fairly easy. However as with learning anything new, some people learn more quickly than others. In this section you will learn various techniques for getting up including the most direct method. If you or your student rider has trouble you'll want to use some of the tips that follow the general instruction. The more difficulty the rider experiences, the more tips on the list you will need to use. You will also learn some tips on how to effectively drive the boat to compensate for rider difficulties. Keep in mind that the driver of the boat is 70 to 95 percent responsible for the success or failure of the first time rider getting up. Now that you know how to equip yourself properly, fit that equipment to your needs, and have a general idea of what to do, you are ready to take the plunge. Get in your gear and get in the water. Start with a rope length of about 50 feet from the center of the boat, or the pylon if you have one. Have the driver idle forward to make the rope tight. The rider should be directly behind the boat. To begin, keep your knees bent, arms straight and head looking up at the boat. Now that you're in position, the driver should begin to idle forward.

As the boat begins to pull, you should begin to sink the tail of the board underneath your body. As you do this, the driver should be paying close attention and begin to accelerate in a firm but controlled manor so that you begin to pop up onto the surface of the water. You must not to begin to rise too soon., and the driver should not exceed 20mph.

If you are using an inboard that has a swim platform at the back, you can practice the following technique before sending a rider out at 50 feet:

🔶 Start by turning the engine OFF. Instruct the rider to put on the proper equipment as if she is ready for a deepwater start. The rider should then get into the water and press the board against the length of the platform. (Fig. 1)

Give the rider the handle and make sure she is in the proper starting position. Grasp the other end of the handle and begin to pull her. (Fig. 2)As you pull, the rider should practice sinking the tail and turning the nose of the board forward as she begins to rise. (Fig. 3)

Make sure that her knees are bent, her arms remain straight and she doesn't try to pull herself up. (Fig. 4)

Common Problems & Solutions
🔶 "When I try to get up, the boat pulls me 'out the front' or onto my face"

Keep your shoulders back as if you are playing tug of war with the boat. Remember, you want the boat to pull you up by the front hip, not by the shoulders. In order to accomplish this, you need to keep your shoulders back and resist the boat while keeping the handle low at your front hip.

● "When I try to get up, the board shoots out in front of me and I fall on my butt"

One or both of your legs are not bent. This symptom is most common when the rider begins to rise. The front leg is straightened and sends the board sliding out in front of the rider. Often, to compensate the rider will pull in on the handle. Both actions are symptoms of each another. Remember to keep both knees bent and not pull in on the handle. This is crucial for success.

● "The rider is pulling the handle to the rear hip as the boat accelerates"
A coach tells of a time when he was proclaimed a genius for pulling this next trick out of his hat. It was his first year of teaching wakeboard clinics on the road. On this particular instance he was in Pittsburgh, PA instructing on the Monongahela River while one of the local shop guys was driving. The student was a boy, of about 9 years old. He had never tried wakeboarding before, so he wasn't comfortable with this new experience and therefore not very confident. The instructor knew that he was limited as to the number of tries the boy would allow before calling it quits. After a couple of tries with the rider directly behind the boat (6 o'clock position), the instructor noticed that he was pulling the handle to his right hip. He was left foot forward, so he should have been moving the handle to his left hip. After this observation, the instructor told the driver to start the rider off at an angle to the boat. The confused look of the driver indicated that the coach needed to further explain that he wanted the rider placed at

the four o'clock position instead of the usual six o'clock directly behind the boat. The driver, still confused began to carry out the instructor's wishes and immediately realized the solution and proclaimed the instructor's genius.

Here is the trick: When the boat pulls the rider at this angle, it makes it very difficult for a rider to pull the handle to the rear hip. The pull of the boat will actually assist in getting the handle to the front hip. If your rider is right foot forward, you will naturally want to reverse the sides and have the rider in the eight o'clock position relative to the boat. As for the boy, he was up and riding after the second try from the angled starting position. Needless to say the driver was ecstatic knowing he had learned a new method of teaching beginners.

Other solutions
If your rider is still having trouble getting up, and you have an extended pylon or a tower, try shortening the line length. This will give the rider a more direct upward pull, allowing the rider to be pulled UP and across instead of just being pulled across, plowing water. Most of the time this simple change will remedy the problem. However, be wary of just how short you make the rope. If you are using an outboard or stern drive (I/O) it is imperative that you use common sense. You don't want the rider, or the rope for that matter, to get chopped up in the propeller. And if you're not cautious of a short rope, you may be putting the rider in the most turbulent area of the wake once the boat is underway.

Up and Riding

The following sections will give you some insight to the basic riding fundamentals needed once you are up and riding behind the boat.

Body Position

The ideal body position for wakeboarding mirrors that of snow skiing, snowboarding or slalom waterskiing - a quiet upper body with shoulders always open to the boat. For those of you who have taken formal lessons in snow skiing or snowboarding, you know a very similar theory - always have your shoulders facing the fall line (the path of which a ball would roll down the hill) In wakeboarding, the fall line is much easier to find, it is the towline to the boat. When you keep your shoulders open to the boat you will naturally keep your upper body "quiet" or motionless. Your shoulders should always be level and not bobbing back and forth. The only time your shoulders will move is when you are trying to get leverage on the boat. (explained in a later chapter) However, keep in mind that this ideal position may take a couple of sessions on the water to get used to.

Approach with sholders open to the boat

Where is the handle?

One of the key elements in this sport is handle positioning. You will find referrals to it throughout the entire book and at training centers everywhere. "Where is the handle?" you should ask yourself this question when learning any and every new trick. When attempting or performing inverted maneuvers and other high-end tricks, you will find that the handle needs to be in different places at different times in relationship to your body. When you are simply riding straight, you will want to keep the handle low, holding it just slightly higher and forward of your front hip. Remember, don't hold or pull the handle up to your chest. (Fig. 1) This will result in you toppling over. (Fig. 2) Think of it this way, when you are playing tug of war, do you hold the rope up high at your chest? Of course not because you'll get yanked onto your face in no time.

You would do much better by keeping it low where your body is not as vulnerable to being pulled over.

It is quite common to see riders who let their hips drop back from the handle, straighten their front leg and have their weight shifted toward their back foot.

This is a poor body position and can be very unstable causing the rider to wobble and fall easily. You can ensure that you don't slump into this position by keeping a slight bend in both knees and shifting your hips forward toward the handle.

Riding with dropped hips

Back and forth inside the wakes

Once you are up and riding you'll want to make sure that you are maintaining the previously described correct body position. Now using your toes and heels, keeping a quiet upper body, move back and forth inside the wakes. Make sure you don't lean in the direction you are trying to go or hunch over at the waist. Remember to always keep your head looking forward at the boat. When you want to travel in the direction your toes face, you should apply pressure to your toes while trying to lift the heels. To move in the opposite direction you'll need to do the opposite, apply pressure to your heels while trying to lift your toes. With practice you will be able to do this without thought or hesitation.

Crossing the wakes

Now that you have an idea of how to get the board to go where you want it to go, it is time to make the bold move across the wakes.

This doesn't require anything new, it's the same basic technique as moving the board from wake to wake inside the wakes, only more exaggerated. Make absolutely sure that you keep your head up and do not look at the wake. Often just looking at the wake is enough to rattle some people and cause them to fall. You will also want to make sure that the wakes are clean and free of whitewash that could scoop up your board and cause you to fall as you cross the wakes. You can "clean up" the wakes by either changing the rope length, increasing boat speed or adjusting the trim (for outboards and stern drives). Try a combination that suits you at a safe and comfortable speed as well as distance from the boat.

To cross a wake, start by going outside the wakes on your toeside. Dig your toes in and cross the right side wake if you are left foot forward. Cross the left wake if you are right foot forward. Maintain your balance by keeping your head up and your knees bent. If you don't bend your knees you may find yourself "slipping" down the other side of the wake and falling.

Continue to travel away from the wake until you are about ten feet from it. Now slowly begin to travel back in toward the wake, again keeping your head up. You are now coming into the wake heelside. Keep your knees slightly bent and continue with your momentum as you travel up the wake.

Stop in the center of the wakes and give yourself a pat on the back. It's a good idea to pause in the center so that you don't take on too many things at once.

Now that you have caught your breath, cut out of the wakes on your heels this time - LFF riders will be traveling left while RFF riders will be traveling right. Remember to keep the knees bent to avoid slipping on the downside of the wake and continue keeping your head up. Once you are about ten feet outside of the wake, begin to travel back towards the wake on your toe edge. Try to avoid hunching over at the waist as you go up the wake. Use your shoulders as leverage to dig in with your toes and edge up the wake.

You will find that it's much easier to edge on your heels than on your toes. Although it is more difficult to edge on your toeside than heelside, it is important to practice and perfect this move early on, as it will help you learn more advanced moves.

Essential Moves

This section will teach you the first basic tricks, which are the building blocks for more advanced moves.

Riding Revert
There are a few different ways to get into the switchstance position
1. Via the side slide or surface 180
2. Via the bunny hop or Ollie 180
3. Via the fakie deep water start

The Side Slide
Start by slowing the boat down to about 15 mph or so, and position yourself in the center of the wakes. Slowing the boat will make it easier for the fin to "release" and let the tail slide out. Remember, the less

you weigh, the slower you will need to go in order for the fin to release. Now, keep your eyes on the boat (head up), arms out, and bend your knees… a lot.

To ensure you're bending your knees correctly, imagine yourself sitting on a chair as you do this trick. Be sure that you are bending your knees and not bending over at the waist. Keep your back straight. While keeping the above in mind, push your rear foot toward the boat. (Fig. 1)

Now, focus on your rear hip twisting toward the handle. The handle should never move during this trick, shifting your weight and twisting your hips in relation to the stationary handle controls everything here. You will need to shift your weight to the very center of the board. (Fig. 2) When you first feel the fin lose its tracking, turn back to your normal position. Repeat this several times. Push sideways and bring it back.

Surface 180 *Notice the handle stays in the same place and the knees are bent throughout the trick.*

You should push the board completely sideways and try to hold it there. Follow through with your initial push so that your toes are pointed toward the boat. (Fig. 3)

When the fin breaks loose it will feel like the board is shooting out from underneath you. Chances are, you will straighten your legs and pull in on the handle. But you will actually need to do the opposite of your natural reaction. Keep your knees bent and arms straight through the entire trick.

Hold the side slide for as long as possible. If you get in trouble during the trick or become tired, bring the board back to your natural position. The main focus to practice and learn is keeping your knees bent. When your knees are bent, the board is underneath you by default. This is a fundamental practice for riders of every ability. As you practice keeping your knees bent during the side slide, you build a muscle memory to always bend at the knees when the board starts to slide out. It will help save you when you start to fall, or get into trouble.

If you find yourself starting to go outside of the wakes, slow the boat speed and keep more weight over your heels.

After you have mastered the side slide you can follow through and bring the board around a full 180 degrees. Simply move your trailing hip toward the handle and put some weight on your leading foot. Magically you are riding revert! (Fig. 4)

Bunny Hop or Ollie 180

Make sure the boat is running at a normal riding speed to work on this move. If the speed is too slow, the water surface becomes mushy, and it is not firm enough to push off or "hop" from. Stay in the center of the wakes with your head looking up at the boat. Practice un-weighting the board with a series of little bounces or hops. This is the equivalent of a mini jump. You won't want to bend down too far at the knees. You will need to bend just enough to get a good spring and pop the board straight up off the water. Practice on land and think about what you are doing to jump. This will help you get it right on the water. Watch to make sure that you are actually pushing off the surface of the water to jump and not just trying to lift your knees. This is a common problem in a failed attempt.

Ollie 180

Once you have the actual hop or "ollie" figured out, all you need to do is turn your back hip toward the handle. The key to this move is to not focus on trying to turn the board 180 degrees in the air. Many riders try to jump too high and bring their knees up to their chest for a full 180 degree turn in the air and then land. The full turn is not necessary and it often looks like sloppy riding. All you really need to do is get the board sideways with the fin out of the water. Once you are at the

sideways position, simply follow through with your rear hip so that it is the one in front. Remember, your chest, shoulders and the rope should never move in this sequence of events. You are only moving the fin out of the water momentarily to transistion into the side slide position. From here turn your hip toward the handle.

Ollie 180 (Cont.)

Fakie Deepwater Start

There isn't really anything new to learn for the fakie start, simply follow the guidelines set forth for a standard deepwater start, but use the opposite foot forward. The mental barrier of getting up revert is the only challenge you will face. Everything else stays the same.

Practice these methods to become familiar with all of them. You will eventually find that you will use the Ollie 180 most of the time to transition into the switch position.

When you are comfortable riding switch, you will need to practice the same maneuvering techniques, such as crossing the wakes, with your opposite foot forward. Following the previously mentioned guidelines should help with this move. Try not to spook yourself; riding revert feels awkward.

The Surface 360

With a little experience riding revert, you are now ready to learn the surface 360. Basically this move is nothing more than spinning around like the hokey pokey behind the boat. The best way to learn this move is in stages, not completing the entire 360 degrees at one time. You will actually break this trick into two separate 180-degree turns.

Start by using the previous trick, riding revert in the center of the wakes (your halfway there already). Let go of the handle with your trailing hand (the one that is now further away from the boat.) and extend the arm that is still holding on.

Surface 360 dry land practice

Make sure that you are holding the handle at the end, not the center of the bar. (Fig. 1) If you are holding with your right hand, keep it to the right side of the handle. When holding with your left hand, keep it to the left side. You will need the extra room when you make the handle pass.

Place your trailing free hand at the small of your back with your palm wide-open facing out. Now look over your trailing shoulder. (Fig. 2)

Now pull the handle to your free hand at the small of your back. As you pull, you should shift your weight the toes of your leading foot. The fin will eventually grab the water and assist the board to rotate. You should turn the handle down toward the water as if you were giving a thumbs down signal (Fig. 3) and continue turning it as you pull in until your hand is facing palms up behind your back.

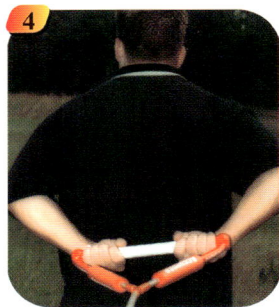

Grab the handle with your free hand and release with the other after you have a firm grip. (Fig. 4) Continue looking over your shoulder until you come around and see the boat. (Fig. 5)

Fly Advice
Keep the leading arm fully extended at the start. You need the entire "pulling distance"

in order to get a complete rotation. If the handle is already close to your body, you have nowhere to pull it, and therefore no rotation will be generated.

Keep your hand at the small of your back. Don't move it from there. Chances are 95 percent that you will move it on the first try. Do not reach for the handle or you are guaranteed to end up with a headache

as a result of catching your heel edge and whacking the back of your head on the water. It happens like this: If your hand moves away from your body to reach for the handle, (Fig. A) your weight will be distributed to your heelside edge which is now the leading edge. At this stage of the trick, the leading

edge will undoubtedly catch the surface of the water and subsequently send you reaching for the aspirin. (Fig. B)

Some riders may manage to keep their hand against their body, but crawl it over toward the other side to place it closer to the handle. The end result here is similar as above, a severe headache. (Fig. C)

Remember to focus on bringing the handle to the small of your back. This is easy to accomplish when you break it down into the following four steps:

1. Get to into proper position: Slower boat speed, riding switch, extended front arm, trailing hand placed at the small of the back NEVER moving until it gets the handle.

3 & 4. Follow through with the turn by looking for the boat and letting the handle pull you around.

2. Look over your trailing shoulder, and pull the handle to the small of your back.

You began the basics of jumping by un-weighting the board when you practiced the ollie. You need to be sure you're totally comfortable with this hopping technique before you attempt other tricks. If you are having problems, keep practicing on land and in the water it until you get it right. One good way to practice the hop is on the edge of a diving board. With just a small bend in the knees, practice a slight little hop off of your toes. The next time you are behind the boat riding your wakeboard, remember the feeling of the diving board and apply it.

One mistake many people make when first learning to jump the wakes is they actually bend their knees too much before getting to the wake. Go back to the basketball court scenario and think about jumping up and touching the rim. Did you bend your knees so far that you were almost squatting? No. Chances are you never wondered why. You should not bend down that far because you will lose the critical timing and energy needed to spring up. After some experimenting, you will find you can get just as high or possibly higher with only a subtle bend in your knees rather than a drastic one. This same theory also holds true on the diving board experiment.

Four Basic Jumps

Like crossing wakes, there are four basic jumps that you will need to learn. You should learn each of them as single wake jumps first by landing in the center (the table), and then progressing to two wake jumps.

Heelside Jump

This is probably the easiest jump to learn. Start it about two feet outside the wake. Remember, you want your back to the wake with your common front foot toward the boat. Now with a slight bend in your knees, turn gradually toward the wake.

Mark sets-up for a heelside jump.

As you ride up the slope, extend your legs and "push" off as you un-weight at the very top of the wake. Think of the slope of the wake as a diving board - as the diving board rises, you begin to extend your legs.

At the very peak of the rising board, your legs should be fully extended. If performed correctly, you will get popped into the air. Keep both hands on the handle during the entire trick for stability.

Drew pushes off at the very top of the wake.

Land in the center of the wake with your knees bent and limber to absorb the shock of the landing. Don't expect to go flying quite yet. You simply want to get the board and the fin out of the water. If you only land on the top of the wake that is fine for now, keep practicing! As you become more stable, you'll want to approach from further outside of the wake. This will carry you a little further across the wake and give you a little more height. You also need to adjust the timing of your pop off the top of the wake as you approach from further out. If you feel you are not getting the pop you once did, adjust your leg extension so that you are pushing off at the very top of the wake.

Make sure you are actually extending your legs straight in the air off the top of the wake. One common mistake riders make is to let the wake push them up. Instead of increasing that force by extending the leg, they actually bring their knees up to their chest.

Toeside Jump
For this jump, you will again start just a couple feet outside of the wake. And of course your toes should be facing the wake on this approach. Using a body position  similar to a heelside jump, where your knees are slightly bent and your back is straight, begin to advance toward the wake.

Bart edges toeside.

Now, pay special attention to the location of the handle. You should keep it close to your front hip, with your back hand simply resting on the handle. Don't pull with your rear arm. Remember, if you jump while pulling with equal strength from both arms, you will be pulled out of position. Extending your legs at the top of the wake, can actually get you a little more pop from

your toes on this side. Be sure you are not looking down at the water. Keep your head looking up at the boat and your shoulders open to the boat. Let go of the handle with your rear hand, only after you land, but before you get pulled out of position.

Heelside and Toeside Switchstance Jumps
Here again, you need to follow the guidelines for standard jumps, but you must mentally prepare for the awkard adjustment of riding switch stance. If you have practiced riding revert as previously described, you should feel more at ease with jumping in this position.

The Double Up

If you're not familiar with the double up, look carefully at the wakes the next time you turn around and drive back through your boat path. The rollers from the path you turn into collide with the wakes directly behind the boat. When the two collide they form a double up. A double up is the brief second when the two wakes form a single wake. A double up can be more than twice the size of a normal wake.

Double Up Driving Tips
Typically, there are three ways to drive the double up. As a driver, you should try to master all of them and then let the rider choose the one that he or she feels most comfortable with. In all cases, be aware that the rider should be approaching the wake heelside from the inside of the loop. This means that for a LFF rider the driver should make a right turn to make the loop,

and a left turn for a RFF rider. Make sure that the loop you create gives the rider enough room to cut away from the wakes without sinking from any slower speeds created from being inside the turn.

🔴 **The standard 90 degree** Like the name says, this method has two paths that intersect squarely at 90 degrees. 1.) Follow a straight path and slow the boat down a little to generate bigger rollers. 2.) Turn 90 degrees to the desired direction and follow another straight path for at least 60 feet. Accelerate to normal riding speed, and hold it through the remainder of the procedure. Several turns can quickly change the boat speed and have a rider attempting a "double up" at close to 30 mph. 3.) Make another 90 degree turn to the same direction and go straight for about 60 feet. 4.) Produce one last 90-degree turn to the same direction and head straight toward the old boat path.

STANDARD 90 DEGREE DOUBLE UP

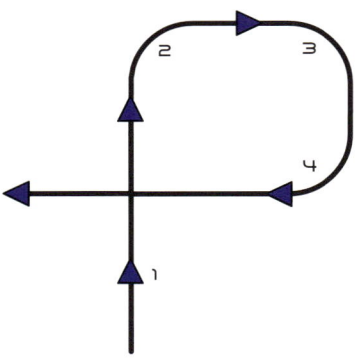

🔴 **The 45 degree** This is preferred by some because it is a little easier to drive, and can be easier for the rider to adjust his timing to the wake. 1.) Drive in a straight

path. 2.) Make a wide turn to the desired direction. 3.) Straighten your path and head for the rollers at a 45-degree angle.

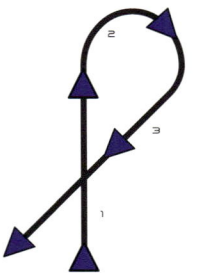

45 DEGREE DOUBLE UP

🔴 **The Super Double Up** This is the monster of them all and has the potential to put you through the stratosphere. There's no doubt it's big, however it has its drawbacks. The super double up is very difficult to drive, hard for the rider to time his approach and results in giving the boat and its occupants a brutal pounding. 1.) Start with a straight path. 2.) Make an arcing 90-degree turn to the desired direction. 3.) Drive straight for at least 60 feet. 4.) Turn the boat slightly again and accelerate slightly above normal riding speed to ensure proper timing. 5.) Make one last wide turn and head directly for the rollers where you made the first 90-degree turn. 6.) Stay slightly to the side so the boat does not smash through the biggest peaks. However, stay close enough so the peaks will still merge with your wake.

SUPER DOUBLE UP

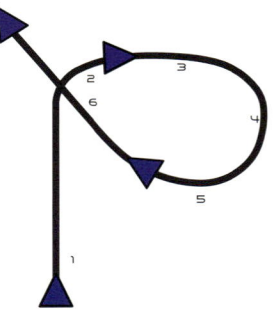

Hitting the Double Up

Hitting the double up requires more skill than driving one. The challenge in hitting the double up lies in the timing of your approach to the wake. If you time it right, you will launch skyward with extra time to

execute a slow, stylish move. If you miss the giant swell, though, you will instead find yourself hitting a giant void. Just as the two wakes converging make a swell twice the normal size, they also create a trough that is twice as deep. By the time you realize you have missed the swell, you have already committed to a move and it's too late. The end result is you in the water. The best advice to help you

hit the double up correctly is to start the approach as you ride over the first incoming roller. It is not necessary to be aggressive when following the swell into the wake. The height of the merging wakes will

send you into the air without a strong cut.

Once you hit the peak your jump, initiate your move in a slow, stalling, stylish manner. If you are doing any type of rotational move, either inverted or on axis, you will need to stall out the rotation by not

pulling in on the handle as hard and opening up your body when you're in the air. Of course, if your goal is to use the extra time in the air to complete more rotations, the stalling will not be necessary.

As you come down for the landing, be sure to have your legs fully extended and ready to absorb a severe shock. Since you are not likely to have much speed coming into the wake, the jump can be compared to an elevator shaft,

5

straight up and straight down. With no speed to displace your downward force, the impact can be much harder than usual, so use extra caution. Landing with your legs locked straight can cause knee damage, and resisting the impact too little will leave you eating your knees and visiting the dentist, all in the same day.

Constant, careful practice will add to your success in proper timing. But, be prepared to occasionally stack (crash), because the double up routinely gets the best of everyone.

Grabs

Now that you have mastered the jumps, it is time to develop some style and start grabbing the board. You should start with the most basic grab, the Indy grab. While in the air, bring your knees up to your chest and grab the toeside edge of the board with your rear hand. Your front hand should be giving a little pull on the handle to advance on the rope and keep you from getting pulled out the front. Try not to bend at the waist. Many riders will try to bend over and reach for a grab. Fight this urge, don't do it! Focus instead on bringing your knees to your chest, and then grabbing the board. If you bend over, your shoulders will get in front of the board and you could find

yourself planting your face in the water frequently. When you look at photos and videos of grabs you will see the riders *are* actually bending at the waist, but they avoid getting pulled out the front by

Todd grabs Indy

tugging on the handle and keeping the board in front of their shoulders.

Skaters and snowboarders should have little problem achieving this style of grab because they have probably done if before. Pay close attention to the following steps involved to grab the board correctly.

1. Approach the wake as you would for a normal jump. (knees bent slightly)
2. Push off at the top of the wake. (straight legs)
3. Pull your knees into your chest and grab. (bent knees)
4. Release and prepare for landing. (straight legs)
5. Absorb the landing. (bent knees)

Grab Don't Slap!
Avoid being mocked by your friends and family by making sure that you actually grab the board. Tapping, swatting and slapping the board don't count. It is far more respectable to take a fall with the board in hand than to crash and miss the grab simultaneously. So, if you see yourself going down, attempt a late grab and use it as an excuse for the fall.

Here is a list of some grabs with brief descriptions to get you started:

Indy Grab	*rear hand toeside grab between feet*
Tail Grab	*rear hand grabs tail*
Tail Grab Nose Poke	*grab tail while straightening or "poking" front leg*
Melancholy or "Melan"	*front hand rear heelside grab through legs*
Method Grab	*front hand, heelside grab*
Roast Beef	*rear hand heelside grab between feet with arm through legs*
Chicken Salad	*roast beef with grab arm twisted, poke out front leg*
Stale Fish	*rear hand heelside grab between feet, arm around back leg*

Jason doing a Stale Fish grab

Rotations

In the following sections, always keep both hands on the handle unless otherwise noted.

Single wake 180's
If you have mastered the Ollie 180, then you already know how to do a one wake 180. The only thing that you need to change is your timing. In this trick, you are simply doing an Ollie 180 off the top of the wake and landing on the table. Start about one foot outside the wake with your knees slightly bent. (Fig. 1)

As you rise up to the top of the wake, give a little pop. (Fig. 2) Once you are un-weighted (Fig. 3), shift your opposite hip to the handle. (Fig. 4) Remember, the handle never

gets pulled or moved from its original spot. Your head and shoulders should face the boat at all times.

The only thing that moves in this trick is your lower body. It's a good idea to practice this on dry land to get a good feel for the "quiet" upper body concept.

Now, try doing the same thing from the other side of the wake starting switchstance and landing with your normal foot forward.

The Next Level

Now pat yourself on the back. If you are comfortable with all the moves, terms and conditions of the previous sections, you have graduated and are ready for the next level. You are no longer at the meager, plebian status of a beginner rider. You have now reached the ever popular "intermediate" level. Don't celebrate too much though, it will be quite a while before you make it through this long stage and into the advanced category. Keep in mind, most riders fall within the scope of intermediate. You are not alone. With some determination and the right attitude, you will become an advanced rider.

The Wake 360

At this point you may think you are beyond practicing some of the basic moves you've already learned. You may be ripping it up doing all kinds of jumps and grabs and think you have no time for beginner moves. Guess again. As promised, the more difficult the moves you are attempting, the more you will need to refer back to the basics.

In order to learn the wake 360, you will need to go back and practice the surface 360. Practice this on dry land with a rope tied to a tree. Continue practicing and make sure you perform all of the key steps to make the move a success. Once the move is permanently burned into your brain, it's time to take it to the air!

Start about halfway outside the wake and approach heelside.

Pop As you get to the top of the wake give a strong push with your legs and get a good pop into the air. It is essential that you do not start the rotation too soon. Make sure you get into the air first. (Fig. 1)

Look Once you are in the air begin to look over your leading shoulder (LFF look over your left shoulder; RFF look over your right shoulder) while your leading hand quickly gets placed at the small of your back. (Fig. 2) The combination of these two motions will initiate the first part of your rotation. Make sure that you are not

hunching over at the waist. In fact it is a good idea to actually arch your back as if someone has a gun to your back saying "this is a stick up!"

Pull Once your free hand has made it to the small of your back, you will need to pull the handle to it as you continue to look for the boat. (Fig. 3) You *pull* the handle. The pull of the handle is responsible for 75 percent of your

rotation. Remember this simple equation as the standard for any type of rotational moves: No pull = no rotation = crash = headache.

After you have made the handle pass, release with your rear hand, and the rope will pull you the remainder of the way around. (Fig. 4) As you complete the rotation, look for the boat. Once the boat is in sight, keep it in focus to stop the spin and avoid over rotation. End with a smooth landing on the down slope of the other wake. (Fig. 5)

To simplify this trick, break it down into a few memorable steps and repeat them on the water. Use the following three, easy to remember words, but make sure you know the meaning behind each of them before you attempt the trick:

1. Pop
2. Look
3. Pull

You may have seen some riders perform the wake 360 with a "half wrap" instead of passing the handle. However this is not the preferred method of teaching because the rope has too much control of the rider. This can be detrimental because it can pull the rider off axis and the rider will not learn how to control the speed of rotation by pulling the handle.

Fly Advice

🔸 If you get off axis push your chest out and arch your back.

🔸 If you are falling over your heels, you are probably reaching for the handle. Remember to pull the handle to your back. Don't try to reach for it.

🔸 Don't bring your knees to your chest. Learn the move the "proper" way first. Once you have mastered it, feel free to experiment with grabs, stalls, and off axis spins.

🔸 Remember, it is usually easier to learn the move by landing in the center of the wakes, especially for lighter riders, or riders who are still having trouble getting across the wakes.

Landing Blindside

Blindside is another term that can be confusing for many who are new to wakeboarding. Although you ride with your opposite foot forward, you are holding the handle behind your back with what is usually your leading hand and your back to the boat. Since you cannot see the direction the boat is pulling you, it is considered riding blind.

Following the guidelines stated earlier, you should start with the most basic moves and build up from there. The most basic move referred to here is the Ollie to Blind. Begin by cutting out a quarter distance from the left wake if you are LFF, and the same distance from the right wake if you are RFF.

Hop the board up and turn the front 90 degrees in towards the wake and release the handle with your rear hand.

As you land, the leading fin will begin to track the board to a revert position. Keep your body weight and shoulders shifted over your toes and more toward your usual front leg. Keep the handle below your waist, but in tight to your body.

After you build your confidence and experience by sliding the board into position from 90 degrees, practice a full 180-degree Ollie turn to Blind. Once you have perfected this move, continue your advancement by jumping from the inside to the outside of the wakes and turning 180 to Blind. Slow the boat down to eliminate any fear and keep your confidence up when practicing wake to wake.

Keep in mind, this is a tough combination to perfect. If you have been paying attention in previous chapters, you should be able to troubleshoot your falls by asking the following question:

How did I fall?

🔸 Over the heels and onto your butt? Solution: Keep the handle low and close to your body. Keep your shoulders over your toes.

🔸 Over the toes and onto your face? Solution: Keep your back straight and don't bend at the waist.

Getting Aggressive

Getting Aggressive

Now that you have some riding experience and are comfortable on the board, it's time to really get down to business and learn the foundations of the most difficult moves. Once again remember, it is imperative that you master these techniques before going any further. The learning process is greatly accelerated by having solid foundations on which to build from.

The biggest key to success with the advanced moves is what's called the "progressive edge". This term is used to describe the proper approach toward the wake. The shortened definition is basically this; after cutting outside (the distance can vary for each move) you initiate a slow, drifting turn back in toward the wake. As you get closer, you'll want to build your "edge". The edge is the amount of pressure put on the rail of the board that is in contact with the water. As you build the edge, you will also create or "load" more tension on the line. Your hardest edge will be at the very top of the wake, where at the last second you push off of that edge and get airborne.

Look at this in a little more detail so that you understand what goes into every part of it. As stated earlier, the distance you go outside of the wake may change for each move, so don't be concerned about it yet.

Understanding the Turn
A basic knowledge of why a board turns will give you some insight into some of the mechanics involved and differences in board features.

A wakeboard is designed to turn as a result of three factors:

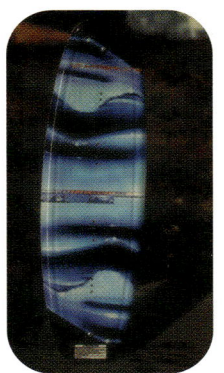

🟠 **Sidecut**
The shape the width of the board follows from tip to tail. Wakeboards have tips and tails that are narrower than the waist. The more dramatic the sidecut, the faster and more "hook" like the turns become.

🟠 **Rocker** This is the curve of the board from tip to tail. The more rocker present, the easier the board will turn. Boards with a large rocker ride slower because they usually plow more water.

🟠 **Flex** The relative stiffness or rigidity of the board. Boards with too much flex ride slow and make it difficult to get a good pop off the wake. More flex will make the board easier to turn.  Boards that are too stiff can be difficult to turn and give the rider hard landings.

Moderation is the key here. Too much or too little of any of the above factors can drastically change the turning properties of the board, as well as many other characteristics.

Progressive Edge dissected

Start by cutting outside of the wake so that you will approach on your heelside. Once you get close to the desired distance from the wake, you will need to slow the board down. To do this you should shift your weight slightly forward on the board. Not only will this slow you down, but also the extra weight on the front will cause the design features of the board to start working by initiating the turn for you. Let the board do all the work for you here. (Fig. 1)

Be careful not to force or "hook" your turn by pushing with your back foot. Make it a slow drifting motion as you transition from your toeside edge cutting out, to your heelside edge coming back in.

Once you are headed back in and have made a complete edge change you should begin to gradually build tension on the line. (Fig. 2) As you get closer to the wake, drop your butt lower to the water and lean your shoulders back. The handle should be pulled slightly in toward your bellybutton. (Fig. 3)

Riders who have ever taken structured snowboarding, snow skiing, or slalom waterskiing lessons will recognize the similarities in body positions throughout the entire process of the turn. In snowboarding and snow skiing, you may remember that your shoulders should always be "open" or facing the fall line. The fall line is the direction a ball would travel down the slope of a hill. This position keeps your upper body somewhat motionless or "quiet" as your lower body goes through all the movements of the turn. For all intents and purposes, the exact same theory holds true for slalom skiing and wakeboarding, until you are airborne. The sequence of events involved with a turn are as follows;

Edge away from the wake on your toes, bend your knees and use your shoulders for leverage on the line with the handle down and in close to your hip.

Initiate the turn by letting your shoulders rise. At this point your body will no longer be used for leverage against the boat. The board should be riding flat, not on edge, and you should push the handle out in front of you slightly. This technique is known as "opening up." Let the board complete the edge transition onto your heels.

Heading back in, begin to bend your knees, drop your butt, pull the handle in and lean your shoulders back into a tug of war position once again.

A good rule of thumb for how hard to edge is to count to ten on your way into the wake, with ten being the hardest edge. Start at zero and gradually edge harder as you get closer to the wake. Your hardest edge should be at the very top of the wake and should be no more than an eight.

Keep in mind that you want to push off of the level eight edge at the top of the wake and as late as possible without totally missing it. Timing the push off the top of the wake is critical. You will find that over the course of your practice, this will often be one of your biggest challenges. Even the best riders can find the timing difficult to gauge.

With these tips in mind, practice your heelside progressive edge without jumping the wakes at first. After you have done that a few times, go ahead and jump the wakes. Make sure that your legs are

Straight legs, tight line, "edging" through the air

fully extended when you are in the air. If your legs are straight while in the air, it's a good indication that you have extended fully off the top of the wake.

When you are in the air practicing these simple wake jumps, pretend to be on your edge through the landing. In other words, keep your shoulders back and maintain tension on the line.

Landing in the flats
At this point, you should be landing well outside of the wake. Believe it or not there are many different ways to land on the other side. The type of move you have done, and the particular style in which it was performed, dictates these different landing styles.

Slow moving, wake-to-wake jumps and moves where you land on the down slope of the opposite wake will result in a smooth, cushy landing. If you were to do this type of straight up and down jump and land a little to far outside in the trough or in the flats, the result would be a hard landing, shin splints, back pain and ankle pain to name a few ailments.

A good example of this theory can be seen by watching big air snowboarding or freestyle snow ski jumping. Ever notice the steep slope that they land on? Better yet, ever gone over a jump while riding a snowboard or skis and landed where there was not much of a slope? Pretty painful, huh? That slope takes the normal shocking impact and displaces the force into energy directed downhill, or in this case down the slope of the wake.

So how do you land way out in the flats without beating yourself up? By carrying speed across the wake and through the landing. As you build your edge, you will naturally create speed across the wake. Make sure that you are on your edge all the way through the top of the wake. If you flatten at the bottom of the wake, you will lose your speed going up the wake and probably come down hard in the trough on the other side. When you land out in the flats, you will want to land only slightly on edge to carry that impact energy into speed. You will notice that when you land with the board flat carrying a lot of speed, the board will tend to "stick" on the landing, and of course your body will continue to move forward and most likely slam you headfirst into the water at a high rate of speed. Remember, when the board is flat, it will ride slow.

Common Problems

Remember, edging hard is different from going fast and out of control toward the wake. When you hook your turns and try to edge too hard too soon, the boat will pull your shoulders over leaving you with no leverage on the boat as you reach the wake. As you hit the wake you will "trip" forward because your shoulders are in front of your toes. The result of this mistake is the infamous face plant which will cost you $7 for a bottle of Advil. If you don't trip over the wake, you will be pulled over the front while in the air and will most definitely smash your face into the water on the other side.

Toeside Progressive Edging & Body Position

Maintaining good body position while getting aggressive on a toeside edge is one of the most difficult challenges that wakeboarders face. Getting it right on a consistent basis takes an enormous amount of patience and dedication. If you have the determination, it is not impossible to master.

Although you will essentially be using the same basic technique explained above, you will need to take some things into special consideration when approaching toeside. The body position starts to get tricky after you initialize the turn in toward the wake, so, make sure your turn is slow, drifting and rounded.

As you begin to head toward the wake, gradually lean harder against the line as you get closer. (Fig. 1) The most difficult part of this trick is to maintain a perfect body position, while progressively leaning harder on the line. (Edging) You should keep a slight bend in your knees with your back straight and shoulders open to the boat, while leaning against the line. Breaking at the waist causes you to rely on the rope for balance. Remember, you should only rely on the rope for leverage, not for balance.

Pull the handle in closer to your front hip as you move toward the wake. Your front elbow should be tight to your body with the entire front arm doing the bulk of the pulling. The rear hand should only rest on the handle. Remember, if you pull with the back arm, you will get yanked off of your edge.

When you reach the top of the wake push off of your toes and as you continue to keep a tight line, lean away from the boat. Your legs should be straight when you are in the air to prove that you extended completely off the top of the wake. (Fig. 2)

You should land onto your toes in the same position you had before you took off, back straight, shoulders leaning against the line and knees bent to absorb the impact. After

you have landed you can release your rear hand from the handle and set the board flat to slow down and recover from the pull of the boat. (Fig. 3-4)

You will need to practice this at the beginning and end of every set that you ride for quite some time before you are likely to master it to the point of not having to concentrate on every step of the move. If you find yourself watching the pros' edge on their toeside, the absolute best to study is Darin Shapiro. Darin's toeside approach is flawless every time, and serves as the definition of perfect toeside body position and approach.

Inverts & High End Moves

General Rules and Principles

At this point, some ground rules need to be laid for inverted moves. You will need to make sure that you are well versed in these principles in order to troubleshoot any problems that you are most certain to encounter while learning the more advanced moves.

One thing that you will figure out by the end of this book is that in general, there are two points at which a rider will fall: in the air, as a result of doing something wrong before getting airborne, or upon landing, as a result of doing something wrong in the air. Either way, you will discover that most of the time it is due to some type of improper position just a few steps before things go wrong. Regardless, by knowing how to categorize your fall, you have already solved the first step in the mystery of "Why did I fall?".

The next thing that you need to be concerned with is the "fly before you buy" program. That is, make sure you have pushed off of the very top of the wake and are in the air, or "flying" before you initiate or "buy into" the move. This can not be stressed enough. It is probably the most common problem encountered when learning advanced moves. If you don't wait until the last possible moment to push off, you are destined to fall in some way, shape or form.

Rotation Principles

You should take note of the next set of interesting rules. If you are already doing inverted and rotational moves you and your friends will have a great time experimenting with some of these general rules of body mechanics.

In wakeboarding, as in other sports, rotational moves are initiated with the head looking in the direction of the desired rotation. Wakeboarding differs somewhat from the others after the initiation and has a slight advantage as well. Other sports rely entirely on body positioning to control the speed and direction of rotation. While wakeboarding does rely heavily on this same principle, the advantage is that a wakeboarder has a firm source in which to assist in controlling these properties, namely the handle. This is why it is so critical to master control of the handle and to keep a tight line at all times. If the line is not tight, you will end up trying to control the rotation with a tool that is essentially not available.

Compare, for example, one specific move in two different sports. The aerial 360 will be the simplest one to follow. Examine this move on a snowboard, which does not use a handle, and on a wakeboard, which does. If you aren't familiar with snowboarding, you might have better luck relating it to the spinning jumps that figure skaters perform. The theory is essentially the same. On a snowboard, a rider initiates the rotation in an exaggerated fashion. That is, the rider not only looks in the direction of travel, but also uses his entire upper body for momentum going into the trick. You can often see a rider "winding up" their upper body coming into the jump, and uncoiling in the air. You've probably seen figure skaters do the same thing. In wakeboarding, this winding up and using your arms and upper body for momentum is unnecessary and will cause you to over rotate and most likely fall. Instead of using the wind up, a wakeboarder can use the handle to control the speed of the rotation. By pulling in on the tight line, the rotation that was just initiated by looking a particular direction is effectively amplified, and is responsible for the rest of the spin.

In other sports and in wakeboarding you can control the speed of the spin after you have already started by changing the position of your limbs. Bringing your arms and legs in closer to your body will increase the speed of the rotation, while opening up, or letting your limbs go loose and away from the body will slow the rotation.

The combination of these two mechanisms gives wakeboarders limitless options when it comes to variations in rotation. Learning how to use these variations will allow you to develop your own personal style.

Fly Advice

- Lead rotations with the head and use the rope for the last fl of the rotation.
- Open your body and let out the handle to slow the rotation; Pull in on the handle and pull your knees up to accelerate rotation.
- Initiate rotations by simply looking in the direction you want to go. Do not "throw" tricks.

- Take one of the previous items and focus only on doing that particular part correctly before and during the attempt. Don't over think the trick before you try it.
- Remember to ask yourself the following questions after each attempt. Where was the handle *actually* positioned during takeoff, mid-air and landing? How were my shoulders *actually* positioned during takeoff, mid-air and landing? Where was I *actually* looking during takeoff, midair and landing?
- Ask yourself how and why you fell. If you fell on your face or over your toes and were pulled forward, you need to keep your shoulders back. If you fell on your butt, you pulled in too much with the handle and/or straightened your legs when you landed. If you fell toward the nose of the board, you may have had a lot of speed and your board stuck to the water when you landed or under rotated. If you fell toward the tail you may have had too much speed mixed with your weight too far over the tail which made your over rotate.

Falling: Attitude and Safety

At this level of riding you will experience severe beatings from the sequential crashes when learning difficult moves. Mentally prepare yourself for the falls by asking yourself the questions mentioned above after every fall. Having this list of questions at the top of your head gives you an immediate task once you float to the surface and will take your mind off of what can be an often frustrating learning process. Sometimes you can get a good laugh if you imagine what your fall looked like to the people in the boat. You should physically prepare for these falls by wearing proper flotation equipment and other body protection such as padded wetsuits. You can also reduce your chances of injury by keeping your arms and legs close to the body instead of flailing around. Try to curl your body into a ball as you roll through your falls.

Trampolines

Trampolines can be a fantastic training tool for wakeboarders, if used correctly. They are great for developing your orientation when airborne or upside down. Doing a proper flip on a trampoline can help you resolve the problem of initiating moves too soon when on the water. For example, if you start your rotation on a back flip (the equivalent of a tantrum) too soon on a trampoline, you will travel across to the side, or possibly off, and onto the ground (ouch). Get your height first. Then, at the peak of the jump, tilt your head back and rotate. When done correctly, you will land on your feet in the same spot you began your jump.

The main disadvantage of the trampoline is that it can be extremely dangerous for both first time and expert users. The other drawback is when you use a handle that is tied to a tree or some other structure, there is no constant pull on the rope to keep it tight. This prevents you from using it as the same tool that it becomes on the water.

The First Invert: Tantrum

"I wanna do flips, I wanna do flips!" This is often something heard from a student who is probably, for the most part, not ready for them. You may even see riders who can barely stand up on the board attempting "flips". This isn't even amusing. The fact is, even though they might be having lots of fun trying these inverts and getting attention for all the entertaining falls from their buddies in the boat, they are not familiar with a basic understanding of how the trick works. If they do not have enough riding experience from learning the basics, they will learn absolutely nothing from their course in repeated crashes. If, on the other hand, you have been riding for a while, feel comfortable with two wake jumps and understand the underlying concepts of the body mechanics previously described, then you are ready to move on to what every rider dreams of getting for the first time: nailing down the first invert.

When you actually ride away from an invert for the first time, it is as if a giant weight has been lifted off of your shoulders. You are now catapulted into a higher level of riding, and if you are the first in your group to do it, the envy of all those who witness. You will of course be quite surprised when you get it. You may find the feeling so strange that your cheering is delayed until you look around and realize your pals in the boat are hooting with fists in the air and cheering you on to do another. Enough of the descriptions, it's time for you to find out what it feels like for yourself.

The Tantrum Defined

The Tantrum is essentially the same motion as a standing back flip. Start by cutting all the way outside of the wake so that you will approach on your heelside. Proceed to initiate your turn, but don't take too strong of a cut to the wake. Although you will need a good deal of speed going into the wake, you will not need much load on the line. Come into the wake with speed, and at the very top of the wake you need to make an edge change and "dig in" with your toes as you release your rear hand from the handle. Turn your shoulders 90 degrees back toward your tracks at the same time. Push off of the kick that you get from the sudden edge change, arch your back, and extend your arm. As you come around, you will need to hang on tight since your arm will be fully extended and the boat will begin to yank you as you land.

The Tantrum is probably the easiest invert to learn, and thus is why most instructors teach it before the other, more complex inverts. It's an easy move because there is not much involved that a rider needs to think about. Basically, if you have done everything correctly through the top of the wake, there is nothing more that needs to be done in the air, unlike with most other inverts. This should immediately tip you off to the fact that most types of falls during this trick are a direct result of improper approach to the wake. Practicing this move on a trampoline can often be effective in learning it properly.

The Tantrum Dissected

Start off with a cut all the way outside of the wake so that you will approach heelside. You will need the distance to generate enough speed to carry you

through to the flats on the other side of the wake.

As you approach the wake, the focus should be on speed, and you will need lots of it. You need a lot of speed for this move because you will lose most of it during the edge change, and you need enough to carry you across to the other side of the wakes. Keep in mind that although you will need a lot of speed, you will not need much load on the line. And therefore you should not edge very hard.

This is the one tricky part, because it requires you to perform three things simultaneously. First, at the very top of the wake, you will need to make an edge change from your heels to your toes. This is a very hard, fast and abrupt edge change. You literally want to be digging in with your leading foot's big toe into the top of the wake. As you do this your head and shoulders should be turning back toward your path by 90 degrees. Let go with your trailing hand while your front hand gets extended as if it became a part of the rope. Approach the edge change like this: Your speeding into the wake and you suddenly decide that you don't want to go across and you want to turn back as quickly as possible. You might want to practice some simple carves off the top of the wake at first. As you get more comfortable with making the edge change, start increasing the distance and speed to the wake. You may also find it helpful to focus on keeping more weight toward your front foot as you come into the wake. This will help you make a quicker change onto your toe edge.

And remember, the more weight placed on your front foot during your approach to the wake, the more the board slows down, and you *will* need speed for this move. Once you come in with a lot of speed and get the edge change right, you will know it. You may be wondering, "How will I know? You will feel it boot you up into the air, and you will probably fall in the center of the wakes the first time you get it right. The momentum needs to go somewhere when you make your stop at the top of the wake and the easiest place for that momentum to go is up.

🟠 Push off of that strong pop or "boot" that you get from the edge change and arch your back. Notice it reads, "arch your back", and not "throw your head back". A couple of problems arise if you throw your head. First, and most likely, it's a sign that you have either A) not gone all the way up the wake to make your edge change and you have done it either in the trough, or in the middle of the wake, and you are trying to compensate for it (even though you may not know it); or B) you did not carry enough speed into the wake and are compensating for it. Secondly, assuming that you got everything else right, it will cause you to over rotate and instead of landing squarely on your feet, you will find the board touching the water for a second before you proceed to fall on your butt. Under rotation is generally not as common a problem so long as you get the pop and arch your back.

🟠 There is not much technique in landing this move. You basically just come around and land as long as you got the first part right

and keep your head up. You may find the handle pop out of your hand a couple times until you get used to the tug of the boat as you hit the water. But for all intents and purposes, when you get the first part right, you won't really need to worry about anything else.

47

Tantrum Variations

Indy Tantrum Go ahead and show some style by throwing in a simple Indy grab with your Tantrum. It's a little easier to get the grab by using a slower approach to the wake and a loftier rotation.

Tantrum to Revert For this one you should actually practice doing a normal Tantrum, only come into the wake with less speed and a rotation that is a little loftier and more "over the top" than usual. You essentially only want to travel wake to wake, and avoid landing in the flats. To start practicing the handle pass and getting comfortable with the 180 degree spin, simply place your free (trailing) hand on the handle as you come down for the landing on a regular tantrum. Practice this until you become very comfortable with the feeling of the spin in the air. Now, instead of simply placing your free hand on the handle, go ahead and grab the handle when you are in mid-air and release with your front hand. Make sure that your head is up and looking at the boat as you land.

Shaun Murray does one of the coolest, most stylish Tantrum to revert around. He's another pro rider who defines perfection for a particular move. His body positioning is so good that sometimes he actually tosses the handle from one hand to another!

Bel Air This is a Tantrum performed without the assistance of a wake. Shaun Murray was the first to do it, and therefore had the rights to name it with a little personalization. Shaun's middle name is Belmont, hence the "Bel".

Whirlybird A Tantrum with a 360 degree spin, pulling the handle over the head for spin rotation. This move is approached similar to a Tantrum to revert, which is slower to the wake, and a snappier flip rotation. This time you will pull the handle in the middle of the flip so that you can see your fist go right over in front of your face. The tension on the rope will actually pull your head and shoulders into the spin as you come down.

Tweety Bird This is another move created by Shaun Murray. Shaun was the guest coach along with Tony Klarich, Andy Lazarus and myself at a Hyperlite Wakeboard tour stop and coaching clinic in Detroit. At the end of the day Shaun went out for a set. At some point someone challenged him to try an Air (no wake) Whirlybird. As usual Shaun was up to the challenge. His first try did not go so well. His second try, he wasn't quite there yet. But never fear, the third time's a charm; He nailed it perfectly along with every attempt following! Needless to say, we were astonished at how quickly he learned the move, and to this day it is one of our more memorable experiences. Oh yeah, in that same set he also was the first to nail an Air (no wake) Scarecrow (also called an "Aircrow") within a few tries as if he had done it all his life.

Rolls

Rolls tend to be a bit more complicated than the Tantrum due to the need for more precise handle control. The easiest of the rolls to learn is the backside backroll, so of course you should start there.

The Backside Backroll Defined

Using a progressive edge to the wake on your heelside, push off at the very top of the wake. Once you're in the air, look up and over your leading shoulder while slightly arching your back. Continue looking over that shoulder and shift the handle to your leading hip as you pull in on the way down. Keep your head up as you land. Both hands should be on the handle at all times!

The Backside Backroll Dissected

⬤ Once you have mastered this move, it is entirely up to you to decide the distance from the wake to start from. For now, you should start about halfway outside of the wake and set up for a strong progressive edge.

⬤ As you come in towards the wake, use your progressive edge to build a load on the line. Keep your eyes focused on the top of the wake as you approach, this will allow you to adjust the timing of your jump, so that you push off as late as possible. Stay on your heel edge with your shoulders back and tension on the line all the way through the top of the wake. As you reach the very top, push off that edge and rise with your body. While pushing off, you should then be looking across the wakes to where you will land. Do not start the rotation yet!

⬤ Only after you have left the wake and are in the air should you proceed to look up and over your leading shoulder to initiate your rotation. Continue to look in this direction until you come back around and spot the boat.

⬤ As you are looking up and over be sure to pull the handle over toward your leading hip while pulling in on it. By the time you pull in on the handle, you should actually be descending, and you may feel as though you won't complete the rotation in time, but remember that pulling in on the handle not only completes the rotation, but speeds it up as well.

⬤ Land slightly on your heels, with your shoulders back and tension on the line. This is basically the same position you started with.

Common Problems

🔹 **Stuffing the nose on the landing**
Although it may be caused by under rotating, it is usually due to not edging through and pushing off the very top of the wake, and not getting enough height.

🔹 **Over rotating** This is usually indicated by the board "popping a wheelie" upon landing. You have most likely pulled in too hard on the handle, or failed to open up to slow your rotation on the way down.

Roll Variations

Backside Roll to Revert / Half Cab Roll
This move is usually easiest to learn at a closer distance from the wake than a normal roll. Start your progressive edge about six feet outside of the wake. Take off as you would with a normal backside roll, looking up and over your leading shoulder, *after* you are in the air. Arch your back immediately after leaving the wake. Midway through the rotation you will need to stop looking over your shoulder and begin to look toward the boat. At the same time you are adjusting your head's position, you will need to let go with your leading hand and open up your body. This combination slows your flip rotation so that you don't slide off your heels and onto your butt when you land. It also enables you to spin the board around 180 degrees to land revert. Since your approach was close to the wake, you should only land just outside of the trough of the opposite wake.

Frontside Back Roll Using your progressive edge on your toeside, edge through and push off of the very top of the wake. After you are in the air, arch your back and tilt your head back slightly. Keep both hands on the handle, but with most of the holding being done by your leading hand (if you pull with your trailing hand you will come down revert). If you

are able to hold the handle into your leading hip successfully, you will have created a massive load on the line. The tension that you have created will transform that slight tilting of the head into a strong and fast spin on the way down, so it is important that you don't throw your head at all, just a little tilt back. Just after you land, release the handle with your trailing hand. If you release too soon, you will not be able to hold onto the yank of the handle with just one hand. If you release too long after you have landed, it is very likely that your trailing arm will get pulled sideways causing you to hook your toe edge, and kiss the bottom of the lake.

Frontside Back Roll to Revert Use the same approach as the frontside backroll, only after you have tilted your head back, tug the handle to what is normally your trailing hip. Keep both hands on the handle at all times. Keep your head up, shoulders back and land on your heels. You may find that this is easier to learn than a standard frontside backroll because of the natural tendency to pull the handle with your trailing hand.

Frontside Front Roll This is similar to the Tantrum, you need lots of speed, but not much load on the line. Come into the wake on your toe side with speed. When you hit the top of the wake make an edge change and dig in with your heels as you push off. You should essentially be smacking the top of the wake with a flat board to give you a "stop and pop" type of jump into the air similar to a tantrum. As you push off, try to force your shoulders up and away from the boat. Now tuck your chin into your chest to start the rotation. Pull the handle into your leading hip to complete the rotation on the way down. Extend your legs to slow the rotation back down, and absorb the landing.

Scarecrow Basically a Frontside Front Roll to revert, however there is a bit of tweaking involved to get it right. You will use the same approach as described previously, with the same edge change at the top of the wake, only on your approach, you should be looking at the opposite wake and behind. Keep staring at this as long as possible. Your head should *not* lead the rotation on this move. After you push off the top of the wake you will twist your leading hip away from the direction that your body is traveling.

You should still be staring at the same spot on the wake. As your lower body twists, pull the handle to your trailing hip, which begins to rotate your upper body.

Your head should be the last thing to come around in a whiplash style at the last moment. You will land revert on your heels with the handle in at your normal trailing hip.

Flips

Flips differ from rolls in that the rotation forces the board end over end (tail over tip) versus a roll's rotation which travels side over side (heels over toes). Its best to imagine a wakeboard front flip as a cartwheel without holding out your arms.

Backside Front Flip Defined
Loading the line and timing your push off the very top of the wake are extremely critical in this move. Take a moderate cut into the wake, push off of your heels and initiate a rotation that sends the board's tail over its tip. Pull the handle into your leading hip to complete the rotation. Land on your heel edge with a tight line.

Backside Front Flip Disected
A medium distance (about 10 feet) from the wake is all that is necessary to learn this move. As you master the flip and the timing

off the wake, you may want to come at it a little more aggressively with some more speed. (Fig. 1) Edge through the top of the wake with your shoulders back, leaning hard away from the boat and keep the handle low. (Fig. 2) Keep your shoulders in this position through the air and the landing.

⬤ Push off of your heel edge and get as much height as possible. Do not initiate the flip yet. Remember that the entire rotation of this move is done on the way down, not up. Keep your shoulders leaning on the line.

⬤ Once you have reached the apex of your jump, tilt your head so your leading ear touches the top of your leading shoulder. If you are using an extended pylon or a tower, it may help to focus on the place where the rope is tied. Make sure that your shoulders are still leaning hard against the line. If your shoulders

go forward, your rotation gets skewed and the board actually does a roll or what is sometimes called a "Frantrum," the combination of a Front Flip and a Tantrum.

⬤ Pull the handle hard into your leading hip with both hands on the handle. Again your leading arm should be doing most of the work so that the pull of your trailing arm does not twist your back end around. While you are pulling the handle in, pull your knees up to help speed the rotation.

⬤ Extend your legs as you come around and spot the landing to stop the rotation and prepare yourself to absorb the shock. Keep your shoulders back and hang on tight when you hit the water because there will be a strong jolting pull from the boat. You should land in the same position that you took off, shoulders back and line tight on your heel edge.

Front Flip Variations

Front to Fakie / Front Half Follow the same rules for the normal front flip, but as you descend and after you pull the handle you must release with the normal front hand, and pull the handle below your normal rear butt cheek. Turning the handle so that your hand is in the "thumbs down" position will speed up the transition to landing revert. Keep your head up and look at the boat as you land.

Raleys

History of the most recognized move in the sport of wakeboarding

The Air Raley gets it's name from one of wakeboarding's top coaches, Chet Raley (Pronounced rāl•ē). Back in 1989, Chet was out on the lake with Darin Shapiro trying to come up with some new moves. Chet suggested that Darin try jumping up and letting his body go straight out behind the boat. Once Darin caught on to Chet's thought, he went out and performed it perfectly on the very first try. Darin chose to name the newly performed move after his longtime friend and coach, Chet. Darin continues to do it the exact same way to this day, and his Air Raley sets the standards by which everyone else's Raleys are judged.

The Air Raley defined

The Raley is like getting pulled out the front, only you push off the top of the wake and get air, which gives you enough time to bring the board back underneath of your body. Use a full length progressive edge, edging through the top of the wake and push off. Instead of

pulling in on the handle, let the boat pull your arms and shoulders forward as the board rises behind you. Keep your head up and looking straight. Pull your knees up to your chest and handle into your belly button for the landing.

The Raley dissected

◗ Cut outside of the wake as far as possible for a heelside approach. Start a smooth progressive edge gathering both speed and load on the line on the way in. Keep your eyes focused on the spot where you will hit the wake.

◗ Edge hard through the top of the wake - about an 8 on a scale of 1 to 10 - Push off your heels at the very top of the wake.

◗ Don't pull in on the handle like you would with other jumps. It is imperative that the line is tight at all times. If you pull in on the handle you will perform a painful, laid out, heels over toes front flip to head plant. Instead, let the rope pull your arms and shoulders out in front of you as the board rises behind you.

◗ As the board rises, the hips and the rest of the body should follow it up. Your body should be totally stretched out with your back arched before you begin to descend. Keep your head up and look straight ahead. If you look down or tuck your chin you will end up doing another heels over toes flip. If you turn your head to either side, you will begin to rotate. As you pull in on the way down the rotation will be amplified and you will land on your side, which is not very fun at this speed and height.

◗ In order to land you must pull the handle in to your belly button and bring your knees up towards your chest. You should land on your heels with some speed out in the flats.

Raley Variations

Hoochie Glide The Air Raley with a Method grab. Take a shorter, less aggressive cut into the wake. As you push off the top, let go of the handle with your leading hand, and grab the edge of the board on the heel side in front of your leading foot on your way up. Of course your body will not be totally extended since you will need to bend your knees in order to grab the board behind you, but you will want to arch your back, and hold the handle with one hand as if you are doing a regular Air Raley. Make sure that

you don't look for the board when you try to grab it. If you turn your head to look for the grab you will rotate, and you have probably figured out by now that rotating during Raleys can be very painful when they are not intended.

Air Kryp An Air Raley with a fakie or switchstance landing. Use the same approach as a Raley. The difference is that on the way down, you will need look over your trailing shoulder and pull the handle behind your butt with your trailing arm as you land. Keep your head up and look at the boat.

S - Bend An Air Raley with a full 360 degree twist while the board is up over the body. This move takes guts and lots of experience with Air Raleys and Front Flips. Use the same set up and launch off the wake like a Raley. Once you have left the wake, instead of looking straight ahead, look up and underneath your trailing armpit. Keep trying to look in that direction, and don't pull in yet! If you have experience with Raleys, you should know that there is plenty of time to pull in on the way down. The same applies here. You need to rely only on your head's position to complete the rotation, so you must keep looking until your rotation is complete and you see your landing through your arms. Only then should you pull in the handle at the very last second bring your knees to your chest and land the trick.

🔶 Start with the board sideways, knees bent, arms straight, and head up.

🔶 As the boat begins to pull, sink the tail of the board underneath your body while turning the nose toward the boat.

🔶 Very slowly begin to rise, making sure that your knees are bent, arms are straight, and your head is up looking at the boat.

Regular Foot

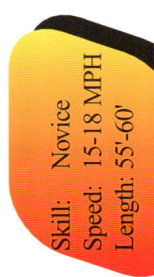
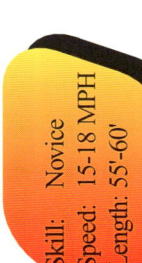

Skill: Novice
Speed: 15-18 MPH
Length: 55-60'

Goofy Foot

Regular Foot

Skill: Novice
Speed: 13-15 MPH
Length: 50' to 65'

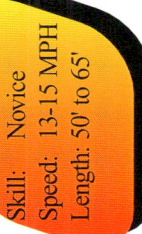

🔶 Start in the center of the wakes with knees bent, arms straight, looking at the boat.

🔶 Keep the handle in the same place as you push your trailing hip and foot toward the boat.

🔶 Continue practicing until you are comfortable with the fin release. Now try to hold the sideslide for as long as possible.

🔶 When you are completley comfortable with the sideslide, follow through to a complete 180 by shifting your weight to your leading foot so that it becomes the trailing foot.

Goofy Foot

Side Slide to 180

Shift weight toward your leading foot as you land so that it becomes your new trailing foot.

Practice small hops, then hop up and turn your trailing hip towards the handle.

Start in the center of the wakes using a normal boat speed.

Regular Foot

Skill: Novice
Speed: 18-20 MPH
Length: 50' to 65'

Goofy Foot

Regular Foot

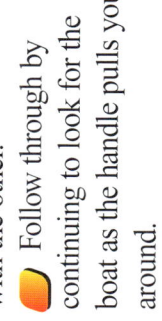

Skill: Novice
Speed: 13-15 MPH
Length: 50' to 65'

🔶 Grab the handle with your free hand and release with the other.

🔶 Follow through by continuing to look for the boat as the handle pulls you around.

🔶 Look over your trailing shoulder as you pull the handle to the small of your back.

🔶 Begin by riding revert in the center of the wakes, extending your leading arm, and place your trailing hand at the small of your back.

Goofy Foot

Surface 360

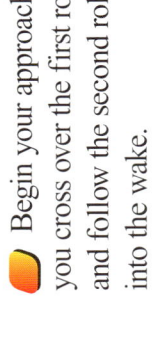

Regular Foot

Skill: Intermediate
Speed: 18-20 MPH
Length: 50' to 65'

▸ Begin your approach as you cross over the first roller and follow the second roller into the wake.

▸ Push off the top of the giant swell where the third roller converges with the wake to form the double-up.

▸ Try to land on the downslope so that your body doesn't get crushed on impact.

Goofy Foot

Single Wake 180

Regular Foot

◗ Approach from only about one foot away from the wake on your toe side.

◗ Unweight at the top of the wake and shift your trailing hip toward the handle.

◗ Focus moving only the lower body while your upper body and the handle stay relativly in the same place.

◗ As you come back down to the water, shift your weight back slightly to your new trailing foot.

Skill: Intermediate
Speed: 18-20 MPH
Length: 50' to 65'

Goofy Foot

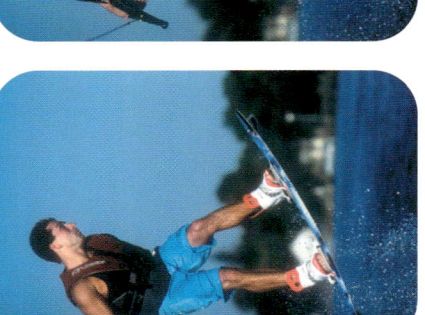

Regular Foot

Skill: Intermediate
Speed: 18-20 MPH
Length: 50' to 65'

Goofy Foot

🔶 **Pop** Give a strong push and get your height before starting the rotation.

🔶 **Look** Look over your leading shoulder while you place your leading hand at the small of your back.

🔶 **Pull** Pull firmly on the handle to your open hand at the small of your back to continue your rotation.

🔶 Complete the rotation by continuing to look over your shoulder until you can see the boat.

65

Keep your shoulders and body weight over your toes, and hold the handle low and close to your body.

As you land, your leading fin will begin to track the board into a revert position.

Cut out to about 6 feet from the wake on your heels.

Hop up and turn the front of the board 90 degrees in toward the wake while releasing the handle with your trailing hand.

Regular Foot

Goofy Foot

Skill: Intermediate
Speed: 18-20 MPH
Length: 50' to 65'

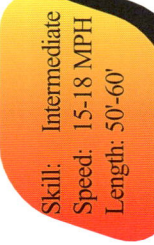

Regular Foot

Skill: Intermediate
Speed: 15-18 MPH
Length: 50-60'

Goofy Foot

🔶 Set up for a heelside approach and cut out just beyond the spray line so that you can generate enough speed to get you to the downslope on the other side.

🔶 Be confident and focus on turning the board a full 180 degrees over the center of the wake.

🔶 Look down over your toes and spot the landing on the downslope of the wake.

🔶 Hold the handle in tight against your waist.

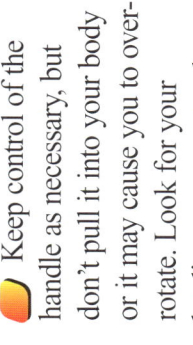

Regular Foot

Skill: Advanced
Speed: 18-20 MPH
Length: 50' to 65'

Goofy Foot

🔸 Initiate a smooth and rounded turn toward the wake on your heelside. Focus on generating speed to the wake instead of loading the line.

🔸 At the top of the wake, dig in with the toes of your leading foot and turn your shoulders away from your direction of travel while releasing your trailing hand, push off and arch back.

🔸 Keep control of the handle as necessary, but don't pull it into your body or it may cause you to over-rotate. Look for your landing as you come down.

67

Tantrum

Regular Foot

Skill: Advanced
Speed: 18-20 MPH
Length: 50'-65'

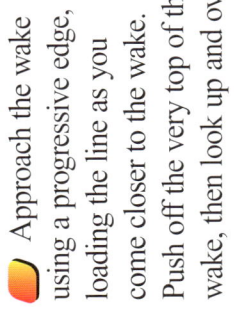

Approach the wake using a progressive edge, loading the line as you come closer to the wake. Push off the very top of the wake, then look up and over your leading shoulder.

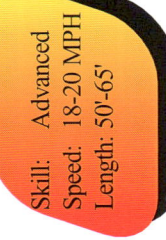

Pull the handle into your leading hip as you begin to descend to speed the rotation and land with the correct foot forward.

Land on your heels with your shoulders back and both hands on the handle, similar to the postiion you had during the initial approach to the wake.

Goofy Foot

Skill: Advanced
Speed: 18-20 MPH
Length: 50-65'

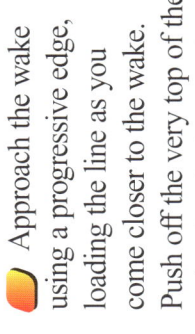

🔸 Approach the wake using a progressive edge, loading the line as you come closer to the wake. Push off the very top of the wake, then look up and over your leading shoulder.

🔸 Pull the handle into your leading hip as you begin to descend to speed the rotation and land with the correct foot forward.

🔸 Land on your heels with your shoulders back and both hands on the handle, similar to the postiion you had during the initial approach to the wake.

Goofy Foot

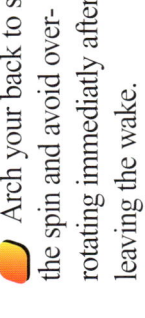

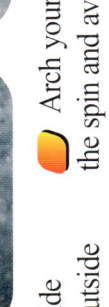

Regular Foot

Approach heelside from about six feet outside of the wake.

Look up and over your leading shoulder, similar to a standard backside Backroll.

Arch your back to slow the spin and avoid over-rotating immediatly after leaving the wake.

Let go with your leading hand, open your body, and look for the boat midway through the rotation. Land revert on the downslope of the opposite wake.

Skill: Advanced
Speed: 18-20 MPH
Length: 50-65'

Regular Foot

Skill: Advanced
Speed: 18-20 MPH
Length: 50-60'

▶ Focus on proper body position as you approach the wake: Shoulders leaning against the line, back straight, and knees slightly bent.

▶ Push off the top and tilt your head back to initiate the rotation. Remember to keep a tight line through the air by leaning away from the pull of the boat.

▶ Release with the trailing hand just after you hit the water to avoid getting the tail pulled sideways.

Goofy Foot

71

Frontside Backroll

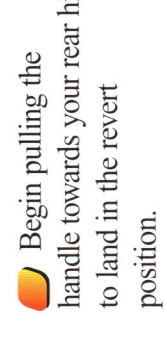

Begin pulling the handle towards your rear hip to land in the revert position.

Try watching the opposite wake until your head gets pulled around to ensure that you are leading the move with the lower body.

Make an abrupt edge change at the top of the wake. Push off and lead the rotation with your hips.

Your front hip should rotate up and away from the wake.

Regular Foot

Skill: Advanced
Speed: 18-20 MPH
Length: 50-65'

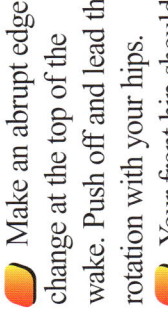

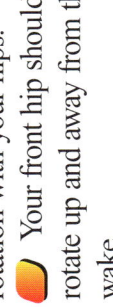

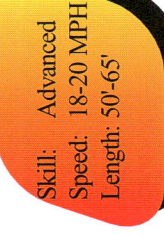

▸ Begin pulling the handle towards your rear hip to land in the revert position.

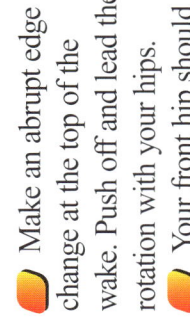

▸ Try watching the opposite wake until your head gets pulled around to ensure that you are leading the move with the lower body.

▸ Make an abrupt edge change at the top of the wake. Push off and lead the rotation with your hips.

▸ Your front hip should rotate up and away from the wake.

Goofy Foot

Skill: Advanced
Speed: 18-20 MPH
Length: 50'-65'

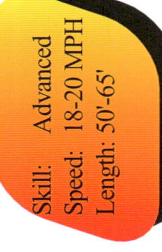

Regular Foot

Skill: Advanced
Speed: 18-20 MPH
Length: 50-65'

🔶 Start only about 10 feet from the wake when first learning this move. As you progress, get more aggressive and take longer cuts to the wake.

🔶 Keep a tight line through the entire move as you push off the top of the wake. Start the rotation by touching your ear to your shoulder and pulling your knees up.

🔶 Pull the handle hard into your front hip to ensure landing with the correct foot forward as you come down.

🔶 Begin to straighten your legs to absorb the landing.

7+

Goofy Foot

Skill: Advanced
Speed: 18-20 MPH
Length: 50'-65'

🔸 Pull the handle hard into your front hip to ensure landing with the correct foot forward as you come down.

🔸 Begin to straighten your legs to absorb the landing.

🔸 Keep a tight line through the entire move as you push off the top of the wake. Start the rotation by touching your ear to your shoulder and pulling your knees up.

🔸 Start only about 10 feet from the wake when first learning this move. As you progress, get more aggressive and take longer cuts to the wake.

75

Front Flip

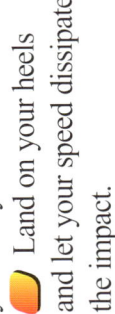

■ Pull the handle in and bring your knees up to get the board back underneath your body.

■ Land on your heels and let your speed dissipate the impact.

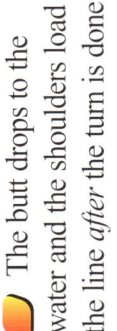

■ Push off of your heels and let your arms get pulled in front of you. Your hips follow the board up behind you until you are totally stretched out. Keep your head up.

■ The butt drops to the water and the shoulders load the line *after* the turn is done.

Regular Foot

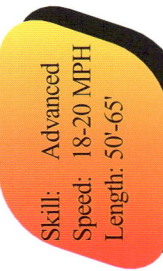

Skill: Advanced
Speed: 18-20 MPH
Length: 50-65'

■ Cut out as wide as possible and make a drifting turn toward the wake on your heelside.

Goofy Foot

Skill: Advanced
Speed: 18-20 MPH
Length: 50'-65'

🔸 Cut out as wide as possible and make a drifting turn toward the wake on your heelside.

🔸 The butt drops to the water and the shoulders load the line *after* the turn is done.

🔸 Push off of your heels and let your arms get pulled in front of you. Your hips follow the board up behind you until you are totally stretched out. Keep your head up.

🔸 Pull the handle in and bring your knees up to get the board back underneath your body.

🔸 Land on your heels and let your speed dissipate the impact.

Air Raley

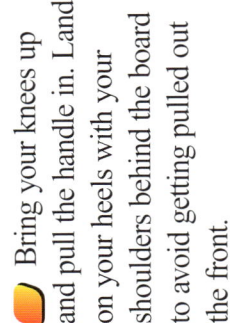

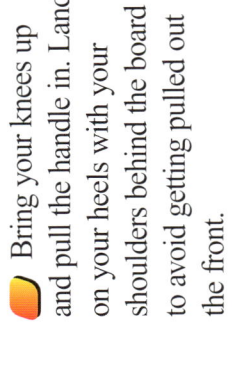

🔶 Bring your knees up and pull the handle in. Land on your heels with your shoulders behind the board to avoid getting pulled out the front.

🔶 Reach for the edge of the board with your leading hand, and keep your head looking forward to avoid any rotation.

🔶 Arch your back at the apex of the jump.

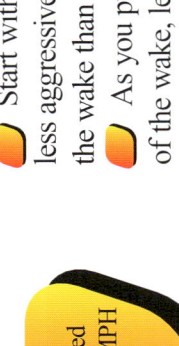

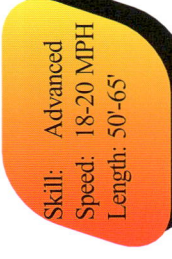

🔶 Start with a shorter and less aggressive approach to the wake than an Air Raley.

🔶 As you push off the top of the wake, let your trailing arm and shoulder get pulled forward over your toes.

Regular Foot

Skill: Advanced
Speed: 18-20 MPH
Length: 50-65'

Goofy Foot

Skill: Advanced
Speed: 18-20 MPH
Length: 50-65'

▶ Start with a shorter and less aggressive approach to the wake than an Air Raley.

▶ As you push off the top of the wake, let your trailing arm and shoulder get pulled forward over your toes.

▶ Reach for the edge of the board with your leading hand, and keep your head looking forward to avoid any rotation.

▶ Arch your back at the apex of the jump.

▶ Bring your knees up and pull the handle in. Land on your heels with your shoulders behind the board to avoid getting pulled out the front.

*Screen shot of **Wakeboarding …On The Edge** interactive CD-ROM*

The CD-ROM Features:

- Fully interactive motion video that you control.
- Videos stop on relevant frames to point out proper body position and further instruction. Continue to play the video at your own pace.
- View the video as a ***mirror image*** instantly, eliminating mental translation for riders using the opposite foot forward.
- Play video without instruction.
- Forward and reverse frame advance feature.
- Cue to previous or next instructional frame.
- Turn music on and off.

Teaches the Following Moves:

- Getting Up
- Up and Riding
- Crossing the Wakes
- Sideslide
- Surface 360
- Heelside Jump
- Toeside Jump
- Double-Up
- Grabs
- Wake 180
- Wake 360
- Ollie to Blind
- Blind Wake 180
- Tantrum
- Backside Roll
- Frontside Roll
- Scarecrow
- Front Flip
- KGB
- Air Raley

System Requirements:
Pentium MMX or higher, 32MB RAM, Windows 95, 98, 2000
Recommended:
Pentium II, 64MB RAM